MY SECOND INNINGS

Praise for *Courting Destiny*

It is not left to every lawyer to command unceasing respect over a period of sixty years. Shri Shanti Bhushan has achieved this rare fame, having started as a pleader in the district courts of Allahabad way back in 1948; and he never looked back after that. My Father late Shri N.C. Chatterjee could see Shanti Bhushanji's immense potential even in those formative years. When some Party approached him seeking his advice on a lawyer for a very complex case, he said, 'If you want glamour, go for Shri... But if you want solid merit, then you can go to a young lawyer, Shanti Bhushan.' Today, I am sure everyone will agree that Shanti Bhushanji has fully justified my father's trust in his capabilities in manifold ways.

During his sixty-year long innings in public life, Shri Shanti Bhushan has endeavoured to strengthen our constitutional edifice as a distinguished lawyer, learned advocate general, a responsible and responsive member of the Rajya Sabha, an efficient and erudite Minister of Law and Justice and a conscientious campaigner for electoral reforms, judicial accountability and probity in public life.

As a legal luminary, Shri Shanti Bhushan has practiced both in the High Courts and the Supreme Court and has won many cases, leaving behind his definitive footprints which have become precedents for posterity. One should mention the habeas corpus case in which his main argument was that the suspension of Articles 19 and 21 of the Constitution did not come in the way of a habeas corpus petition. He contended that even when fundamental rights did not exist, a habeas corpus petition was maintainable.

He effortlessly combined his legal and judicial acumen with the finest tenets of parliamentarian behaviour during those eventful days. I recall with a sense of profound appreciation the consummate skill and the conviction with which he piloted the historic 44th Constitution Amendment Bill which removed from our organic law the provisions of the 42nd Amendment Act, which has tarnished our Constitution. Vigilant people like Shri Shanti

Bhushan fought courageously against the stifling of dissent and democracy during the internal Emergency to put the nation back on the right track. Shri Shanti Bhushan is not only an illustrious legal practitioner, but also an activist lawyer. His sustained campaign to reform the judiciary of the several ills afflicting it is highly commendable. He has also been a champion of judicial accountability about which much is talked about these days even in the highest judicial circles. In this context, I recall the occasion when we met in connection with the petition against Justice Ramaswami seeking his impeachment and how he campaigned vigorously to ensure that the process was not derailed because of political reasons. The memoir is not only biographical in nature but is also a chronicle of contemporary India...I am sure, the book will rightly be treated as authentic source of information for researchers and the intelligentsia. With these words, I have great pleasure in commending his memoirs to the readers.

—Somnath Chatterjee, former Hon'ble Speaker, Lok Sabha

Courting Destiny: A Memoir is an autobiography by a distinguished lawyer who has always been guided by his convictions. It is the journey of Shanti Bhushan's life predominantly through the legal cases that he has argued. Even his critics would concede that the author is a man wedded uncompromisingly to his convictions. He is unwilling to bend. Compromise for convenience or pragmatism ahead of conviction is unknown to him.

—Arun Jaitley, Minister of Finance and Corporate Affairs, India

Whether Shanti Bhushan courted destiny, or destiny courted Shanti Bhushan is part of this engaging memoir which is personal, proud, elegant, exacting, prejudiced and nuanced... Shanti Bhushan's account is frank and fearless. He has his own sense of humour and his vanities. But that does not prevent this book from being an engagingly marvellous account of his private and public life.

—Rajeev Dhawan, Senior Advocate

I can imagine that this book will become compulsory reading for all young people who choose the legal profession in India. It captures the flavour of the courtroom: the drama, the clash of ideas and personalities, the impact on the lives of people and nations, even the intrigues and pettiness. He is a tall man in many ways...in his intellectual brilliance, his learning, his integrity, his professional prowess and the courage of his convictions.

—Harsh Mander, Activist

MY SECOND INNINGS

SHANTI BHUSHAN

RUPA

Published by
Rupa Publications India Pvt. Ltd 2018
7/16, Ansari Road, Daryaganj
New Delhi 110002

Sales Centres:
Allahabad Bengaluru Chennai
Hyderabad Jaipur Kathmandu
Kolkata Mumbai

ISBN: 978-93-5333-270-9

First impression 2018

10 9 8 7 6 5 4 2 3 1

The moral right of the author has been asserted.

Printed by Gopsons Papers Ltd., Noida

CONTENTS

INTRODUCTION

My memoir, *Courting Destiny*, was released by the late Somnath Chatterjee, former Speaker of Lok Sabha, on 11 November 2008, which was my 83rd birthday.

At the age of eighty-three, I thought that I had played my last innings and nothing of significance was now going to take place in my remaining life. And thus, *Courting Destiny* was to be regarded as my complete autobiography.

However, it seems now that the destiny which had been courting me had different plans and the events which took place after 11 November 2008 were even more exciting in my life than those which had taken place prior to that date. My fight with judicial corruption in which I filed an affidavit in the Supreme Court stating that eight out of the sixteen retired Chief Justices of India were definitely corrupt; the 'Anna Andolan' that took place thereafter which shook the country was responsible for the decimation of the Congress Party in the next parliamentary elections; the formation of the Aam Aadmi Party, its grand success in the Delhi legislative elections, and thereafter, Arvind Kejriwal's betrayal of all the founding principles of AAP, and turning the same into a corrupt and totally unprincipled organization—all took place after the publication of *Courting Destiny*.

These were very significant events in my life. Some epoch-making cases in the Supreme Court also happened in which I played an important role. I was, therefore, advised by my friends that I should write a sequel to my memoir narrating these events. I pondered over the suggestion and was reminded of a cricket Test match between India and Australia in March 2001 in which India played a historic second innings after being destroyed in the first. Australia batted first and scored 445 runs and was also able to dismiss India in their first innings for a paltry score of 171, thus getting a first innings lead of 274 runs. The Australian captain expected an Indian defeat, but incredibly, in the second innings, thanks to the batting of V.V.S. Laxman and Rahul Dravid, they were able to score 657 runs after losing only 7 wickets and set Australia a target of 374 in 74 overs. The Indians were also able to dismiss the entire Australian team in the second innings for a meagre 212 runs, and thus snatching an incredible victory by 171 runs.

On remembering this match and comparing India's second innings with their first, it seemed to me that sometimes a person's second innings may be more interesting than his first. I, therefore, agreed to the suggestion of my friends to write about my experiences in the second innings after the age of eighty-three and decided to name it *My Second Innings*.

I also pondered over the thought that maybe rather than another memoir I should have just listened to the poet 'Akbar Allahabadi', who had once said that an autobiography should be written in just nine words:

'BA hue, naukar hue, pension mili, phir mar gaye.'

Got the BA degree, got a job, retired, got pension and then died.

However, it is now too late.

1

19 ELGIN ROAD:
THE BHUSHAN HOME IN ALLAHABAD

My father, Vishwamitra, had started his practice in Meerut in 1916, where he had done his B.A. L.L.B. A year later, he decided to return to his hometown, Bijnor, to practise law there and rented a house to live in. At one point, he decided to have that house painted according to his own tastes but did not consider it necessary to take permission from the landlord to do so, who resented this violation of his rights when he found out about it. The landlord then asked my father to vacate the house. Vexed by this experience, my father decided that he must have a house of his own. There was one on sale in Mohalla Balmuknd, whose owner lived in Meerut. My father, enterprising as he was, left immediately on his cycle for Meerut to meet the owner. He cycled overnight and reached Meerut next morning, where he met the owner and settled the purchase of the house for about ₹3,000, which due to his frugal habits he had been able to save from his income as a lawyer. Upon his return, he settled down happily in a house that was truly his.

In 1927, on being urged by his youngest brother, Anand Mohan, he decided to take the plunge and shift to Allahabad to practise in the High Court. Allahabad at the time was not only the seat of the High Court but also a great educational centre with the best university in the country, which was then known as the Oxford of the East. Of the many reasons that my father had for making that move, the most important one was the education of his children.

Without making any prior arrangements in Allahabad, my father boarded a train for the city with his wife, three children, my uncle, and a close family friend and a lawyer, Nemi Saran Jain. On reaching Allahabad, we checked into a dharamshala. A little later, my mother cooked food for my father, Nemi Saran, my uncle, and us children. After which they hired a tonga and left in search of a house in the city's poshest area—Civil Lines. Rents being quite high there, houses were lying vacant with signs of 'To-Let'.

Between 1927 and 1939, we lived in several houses as tenants, and then finally in 1939, we moved into 19, Elgin Road.

Before we moved into this large house, it had been lying vacant for more than fourteen months after Shri Kamala Kant Verma had vacated it after he became a judge in the High Court in 1937. But the rent he had been paying was ₹185 per month. The rents had been falling in the city and nobody was prepared to take that house at that price. So, it remained vacant for long. The owner was the biggest landlord of Civil Lines; he owned almost fifty houses. In fact, many of the European judges were his tenants.

After losing out on rent for fourteen months, the landlord reduced the rent and negotiated with my father and both agreed on ₹140 per month. My father made a condition that a large inner courtyard with walls on all sides would be built as well as a new kitchen complex and a verandah where his children could sit and eat. This too was agreed upon by the landlord Manmohan Das

Tandon, popularly known in Allahabad as 'Bachchaji'. We happily shifted to this very large house in April 1939, a few months before the Second World War began.

Sometime in 1946, my father received a legal notice from a lawyer named Shyam Nath Kakkar who, we found, had just been enrolled as a pleader at that time. Many years later, we went on to become close friends, and in 1977 when I became Law Minister in Morarji's Cabinet, I appointed him as the Solicitor General of India.

The legal notice stated that the rent control law provided for a 25 per cent increase over the pre-war rent and as Kamala Kant Verma had been paying a rent of ₹185 per month, it had to be increased by 25 per cent to ₹231 per month. We looked up the law and found it to be almost true. The law provided that the landlord could increase the rent to an amount which was 25 per cent above the municipal-assessed rent of 1942. But the municipal-assessed rent in 1942 was only ₹110 per month and so, the legally permissible rent was only ₹137.50 per month and we were already paying more than that, ₹140 per month to be precise. Hence, a reply to the notice on these lines was sent.

Shyam Nath Kakkar then filed a suit in the Civil Court for fixation of the rent at ₹231 per month. We contested the suit and the judge began recording the evidence. When the chief witness for the plaintiff landlord appeared as a witness, he was asked in a cross examination by our counsel, Jagnandan Lal, that if the rent earlier was so high, why was the house let out to the defendant at the low rent of ₹140 only. His reply was that as the defendant was a high-class Brahmin, the landlord, who had great respect for Brahmins, wanted to help Vishwamitra. Probably, the witness confused my father with the great sage Vishwamitra in Hindu mythology.

The judge was quite amused as he knew that my father was a Baniya and not a Brahmin at all. He finally dismissed the plaintiff's suit. No appeal lay in that suit for fixation of rent. So, Shyam Nath Kakkar got a revision filed in the High Court.

The revision came up for admission hearing before Justice Bind Basini Prasad, who had been a munsif in Bijnor when my father was practising there. Seeing my father's name as the respondent, he asked, 'Is it our Vishwamitra?' On being told that it was indeed so, he allowed the revision to be admitted for hearing.

After some time, the case came up for hearing before Justice Bhargava where I represented my father as his counsel. Vashisht Bhargava was my father's student in Government High School at Meerut where my father taught from 1914–16 and studied law himself in evening classes. Bhargava's father was the headmaster of that school. I had once jokingly asked my father whether he had ever caned Bhargava. He said that that never happened as Bhargava was not only a very good student but also a very well-behaved one.

After hearing both the sides fully, Justice Bhargava dismissed the revision finding no merit in it. This was sometime in 1956.

I got married in 1955, and one evening, when I returned from the High Court in the evening, I was greatly surprised by the reception I got. My parents were ready for aarti, with a large steel thali comprising a silk sari and gold ornaments for my wife Kumud, a decent present for me, along with sweets and dry fruits. I was told that this was my 'shukrana' for winning the case.

The 19, Elgin Road house has had a great history for our extended family for the last seventy-eight years, with decades' worth of memories attached to it. We have even hosted several family weddings in that house, including my own in 1955—in which, due to heavy rains, the large shamiyana had collapsed and the party had to be shifted indoors and yet it was attended by more than 800 people.

We also hosted several important politicians in that house. When former chief minister of Karnataka, Shri Nijalingappa, came to give evidence in Raj Narain's Election Petition against Indira Gandhi, I received him at the airport and brought him to 19, Elgin Road. Upon entering our large drawing room with the high ceiling, he had asked, 'Is this the Government House?' and I replied, 'No, this is the Opposition House.'

Two former prime ministers—Morarji Desai and Charan Singh—have also stayed there; in fact, Morarji insisted on washing his own undergarments during his stay. Sucheta Kriplani and Acharya J.B. Kriplani, Shri Ashok Mehta, Maharani Patiala, Sardar Patel's daughter Maniben Patel, the irresistible Tarkeshwari Sinha, C.B. Gupta, Ram Subhag Singh, and many others stayed at our house. And those who have dined there with us include Piloo Mody, Rabi Ray, Shyam Nandan Misra, and many others. I can confidently say that after Motilal Nehru's Anand Bhavan, our 19, Elgin Road has seen more political history than any other house in Allahabad.

Our house was built on a plot of about three acres in Civil Lines in Allahabad. It had about two dozen large outhouses for servants. As I had three uncles who were in senior government positions, and had transferable jobs, my father had insisted that their children also stay and study with us in Allahabad. Therefore, there has always been a deep bonding among us cousins. My sister is now ninety-four years old and I too am in my ninety-third year. Many of my cousins who lived with us in the house for considerable periods are also nearing their eighties and nineties. They fondly remember their stay at 19, Elgin Road as the whole family had developed a great attachment to this house.

Sometime in the 1950s, the ninety-year-old lease of this house in favour of the landlord from the government had expired and the efforts for its renewal were going on. My father, who was very keen to purchase the house, but was never able to save enough money to be in a position to do so (which would have then cost anything from ₹30,000 to ₹40,000), continued to live as a tenant.

Once I had established my practice as a lawyer, I decided to purchase that house. And thus, I entered into an agreement with the landlord. On 2 September 1966, it was agreed that after the landlord was able to get the government lease renewed for another ninety years, he would sell the entire property to me for a total amount of ₹100,000. I paid him an advance of ₹5,000 with a cheque at the time of the agreement. The balance amount was to be paid at the time when the sale deed was executed after the extension of the government lease.

Thereafter, news was trickling that the government may not renew the lease for the entire three acres. So, we entered into a fresh agreement on 25 April 1970 in which it was stipulated that if the lease was renewed for one acre of land with the main bungalow, the price payable by me to the landlord would be ₹48,000, and in case the lease was renewed for the land of more than one acre, the rate of such extra land over one acre shall be ₹30,000 per acre. One of the terms of the agreement was that the landlord would get the leasehold rights renewed for a further period of ninety years and execute the sale deed in my favour or my nominee's favour after taking the balance sale consideration.

The question of renewal of lease remained pending for a long time and since after expiry of the lease deed, the landlord did not have any transferable right, the sale deed could not be executed. It was in the year 2000 that the government took a final decision about the lease deeds in Allahabad's Civil Lines and decided that they would renew the deeds on a freehold basis by charging some additional premium for freehold rights. The landlord, therefore, got a freehold lease from the government on 8 June 2000.

By this time, the prices of property had risen and, therefore, the landlord was not ready to honour the agreement of 1966 or 1970. I, therefore, filed a civil suit in the year 2000 against him for specific performance of the agreement in the Court of Civil Judge, Allahabad. As the courts in UP were highly congested, the case continued to drag on and even the issues had not been framed by the year 2010.

As I was approaching my eighty-fifth birthday, I was not sure how much longer I was going to live and was keen to fulfil my father's wish to get the house registered in the name of the family, in my lifetime.

Some brokers suggested that the matter could not be amicably settled unless I was willing to give up my claim on about one-third of the land. I thought about it and, in spite of the fact that I had a cast-iron case in the suit for specific performance, I felt that the litigation might continue for another decade or more and it would be advisable to enter into a compromise. So, I decided to agree to the suggestion and gave up my claim on about one of the three acres of the land which was an open area and could be commercially exploited by the landlord. A fresh agreement reciting all these facts was executed between me and the landlord on 12 October 2010 which stated that a compromise had been arrived at between the parties, and the landlord had agreed to execute a sale deed for 7,818 sq. metres of land along with construction and substructures standing thereon which included not only the main building but also a cottage which was in the occupation of another tenant.

The compromise was filed in court and a decree was passed on 16 October 2010 disposing of the suit on the basis of the compromise. The landlord had agreed to transfer the 7,818 sq. metres of land, roughly about two acres with the main bungalow as well as the cottage and all the outhouses, for the originally agreed amount of ₹100,000 out of which ₹5,000 had already been received by him at the time of the agreement in 1966 and, therefore, a balance of ₹95,000 was to be paid to him. After the decree for specific performance was passed for this property according to the agreement, the sale deed was executed and registered. Thus, our family became the owners of the property in which we had been living since early 1939.

My father was of a very helpful nature. Therefore, even distant relatives in distress who came to Allahabad were accommodated by him in the various outhouses after renovating them, and they continued to live there generation after generation. Similarly, when a servant, who had been living in one of our outhouses died, his family was allowed to live in the same quarter without paying any rent.

An important question arose at that time as to what was the stamp duty payable on the sale deed. The stamp duty payable as per law was an advalorem duty on the market value of the property conveyed. The question was how this market value of the property conveyed was to be assessed.

The landlord had very limited rights in the property as most of the rights continued to remain with the tenant by the various statutes which had been enacted in UP. The landlord could not evict the tenant except on certain grounds like non-payment of rent or damaging the property, etc.; he could not even increase the rent. As our landlord was a well-known one in Civil Lines and was the owner of many properties, which were occupied by tenants, it was also not possible to have any of these properties released in his favour under the law for personal need. There were a large number of cases which laid down that where the property was covered by Rent Control Legislation (which prevented an increase of rent as well as restricted the eviction of tenants), the market value of the owner's rights had to be assessed merely by capitalizing the rent he was receiving or was entitled to receive under the law. We, therefore, calculated the market value on that basis and even adopted the municipal assessment rental value rather than the rent payable by us and paid the stamp duty thereon. This was in October 2010 when the sale deed was registered.

In April 2011 when the first phase of the Anna Andolan demanding a Joint Drafting Committee for the enactment of the Lokpal Bill was in full swing, the ruling Congress Party was out to destroy the image of the civil society members of the Drafting Committee—which included me. They had asked for the declaration of assets by the civil society members of the Drafting Committee and we had all made that declaration, in which all properties owned by us were shown, including my Allahabad house. So, the ruling party members got a notice issued by the stamp authorities on 15 April 2011, indicating a deficiency of advalorem ₹13,379,000 in the stamp duty paid. Therefore, they started propagating that I had consciously tried to defraud the stamp authorities of the proper stamp duty payable on the sale deed. The matter was contested before the stamp authorities; but they decided that the market value had to be determined by taking the value of the land which had been released in favour of the landlord and which, in the meantime, had been sold by the landlord to various parties. Therefore, they laid a charge against me that I was attempting to defraud the stamp authorities. This matter of the proper stamp duty is now pending in the Supreme Court in which leave under Article 136 has already been granted by the Supreme Court in July 2017, and the appeal would come up in due course.

We have an unassailable case as the various decisions of the Court show. However, the whole family, including the extended family, is happy that we are now owners of 19, Elgin Road and the family will continue to enjoy the same and remember the old events which took place in that large house.

2

BATTLE AGAINST JUDICIAL CORRUPTION

Even more pernicious than delays is the corruption pervasive in the judiciary. There may be a difference of opinion on the extent of corruption at different levels of the judiciary, but those lawyers and litigants who deal with the courts have not the least doubt that corruption exists in the judiciary at all levels—from the lower courts to all the way up in the Hon'ble Supreme Court of India.

Many distinguished Delhi District Court lawyers come and tell me that at least 80 per cent of the judges in the Subordinate Courts of Delhi are not totally honest. While they may not be taking bribes in every case, they are quite prepared to take a bribe in important matters where a client can pay them a decent sum for a verdict in his favour. Even in the High Courts of the country, there are plenty of black sheep, but since no effective action is being taken to deter them from engaging in corruption, the malady keeps growing. It is a similar situation with the Supreme Court, where there are undoubtedly many excellent judges who are totally incorruptible and honest, but it cannot be said that even the apex court has remained untouched by corruption.

In 2001, a Delhi-based magazine called *Wah India* embarked upon a noble idea of judging judges of the Delhi High Court.

They circulated a questionnaire among fifty senior lawyers, which at that time was 10 per cent of the total strength of the Delhi High Court Bar. This questionnaire evaluated the judges on their integrity, understanding of law, and courtroom behaviour, among other things. The questionnaire was to be answered anonymously so that the advocates could freely answer the questions without any fear of reprisals from the bench. After receiving the filled-out forms, *Wah India* published a chart in their magazine showing as to how the different judges of the Delhi High Court had fared in that assessment. This created a big furore at the High Court and Madhu Trehan, the editor-in-chief of the magazine, had to promptly issue an apology after being served with a contempt notice. In the end, this unique experiment was nipped in the bud.

It is a well-known fact that the lawyers practising in a court have a fair idea as to whether a particular judge is corrupt or not. If the highest people in the judiciary were really interested in finding out whether judges are corrupt or not, they should use the *Wah India* experiment for the assessment of all the members of the Bar who have been regularly practising in those courts. While this is obviously not conclusive, but it certainly does give a reliable direction to find where the corruption lies in the judiciary.

Even those people who have known about judicial corruption at first-hand are afraid of speaking up because of the contempt power which has been wielded by the courts from time to time. I strongly believe that public pressure can serve as a deterrent to corruption.

On 5 September 2009, *Tehelka* magazine interviewed Prashant Bhushan[1] when he had succeeded in making judges agree to declare their assets. In the interview, Prashant lauded

---

[1] *Tehelka Magazine*, Vol. 6, Issue 35, 5 September 2009.

the judges for relenting and declaring their assets and gave a specific example of how that can deter corruption. He said that if tomorrow a judge omits to declare a property (ostensibly ill-gotten wealth) then there is a chance that someone might know about these particular properties and blow the whistle. One could then examine if these can be explained within their legal income, and if nothing else, it certainly shows the point of public pressure. Prashant further mentioned that there were two watershed events—the Chief Justice Sabharwal case (where there was an allegation that Y.K. Sabharwal's orders to demolish commercial outlets in Delhi directly benefited his sons, who were partners with certain mall developers) and the Ghaziabad Provident Fund scam. Both these cases received wide media attention.

A 2006 Transparency International report said that the judiciary in India is the second-most corrupt institution after the police. On being asked about the impeachment of judges of the Supreme Court, Prashant said that despite credible evidence there have been no such successful impeachments like in the case of Justice Ramaswamy, Justice Punchi, and Justice Anand, who all then went on to become chief justices of India. Prashant went on to mention that today impeachment is impractical. To move an impeachment motion you need the signatures of 100 MPs and their decision to join in is very political. For example, in the impeachment proceeding against Justice Bhalla, the BJP declined to sign because L.K. Advani had been acquitted by him in the Babri Masjid demolition case.

In addition to the impeachment route, there is an in-house procedure that was set up in 1999, post a chief justices' conference in 1997, but that too is activated only selectively. For instance, the complaint against Justice Bhalla was that he had purchased land worth ₹4 crore at ₹4 lakh approximately from the land mafia in Noida. This was based on a report from the DM and SSP of Noida. This land mafia had several cases pending in courts subordinate to Justice Bhalla. Another complaint was that in the Reliance Power matter, though his son was the lawyer for Reliance Power, Justice Bhalla constituted a special bench while he was the presiding judge in Lucknow. He sat in the house of one of the judges at eleven in the night to hear their case and passed an injunction in their favour. I asked Chief Justice Sabharwal to initiate proceedings against Bhalla, but he refused. Similarly, Justice Vijender Jain presided on the case of a person whose granddaughter had been married out of his own house. He was a close friend of Jain's, but he still heard and decided the case in his friend's favour. In such cases, although very specific complaints were made to the then Chief Justice of India (CJI), he didn't do anything to activate the in-house procedure. All the judges mentioned above have gone on to become chief justices; Bhalla went on to become the Chief Justice of the Raj High Court and Virendra Jain became Chief Justice of Punjab and Haryana.

Prashant went on to say in that interview that what is needed is an independent institution for entertaining complaints and taking action against judges. There has to be a National Judicial Complaints Commission—independent of the government and judiciary. It should have five members and investigating machinery under them. The second problem lies in the Veeraswamy judgement, which ordered no criminal investigation can be carried out against a judge without prior written permission of the Chief Justice of India (CJI). That's what happened in Karnataka: There was a complaint against several judges visiting a motel and misbehaving with women. When the police officer came, the judges threatened him and said no FIR could be filed against them because they were judges. The same happened in the Ghaziabad Provident Fund case as well—the investigation of which is stymied because the CJI did not give the permission. We have to get rid of this injunction. And the third problem is the Contempt of Court Act. Today, even if you expose a judge with evidence, you run the risk of contempt. Judges are even seeking to insulate themselves from the RTI. We have to get rid of certain parts of the Contempt of Court Act. Only specific parts of it should go and not the whole Act. For instance, disobeying the orders of the court is civil contempt—this should stay put; interfering with the administration of justice is criminal contempt—this should also stay. What needs to be deleted is the clause about scandalizing or lowering the dignity of the court, something for which even author Arundhati Roy was sent to jail.

Finally, there is the problem of appointments. Earlier, judicial appointments were made by the government, which was bad enough. Now, by sleight of hand, the Supreme Court has kept the power of appointments to itself. Earlier, there were political considerations; now there are nepotistic ones. And this can be solved by having an independent Judicial Appointments Commission, which is independent and works full-time, and follows some systems and procedures. Eligibility lists should be prepared and comparative merits debated and evaluated. You can't just pick judges arbitrarily, and let people know about it only after the deed is done.

Prashant went on to give another example of judicial impropriety. Justice Kapadia who decided on the Niyamgiri mining lease case in Orissa had said that Vedanta can't be given the lease because it's been blacklisted by the Norwegian government; but its subsidiary company Sterlite can get the lease because it is a publicly listed company. The issue here is that Justice Kapadia should have recused himself from hearing this matter because he was a shareholder in Sterlite.

In the entire interview the statement which got the most

publicity was the one where Prashant said that in his opinion of the last sixteen chief justices of India, half were corrupt. Shortly thereafter, Shri Harish Salve as Amicus Curiae, made an application to the Supreme Court against Prashant Bhushan and Tarun Tejpal, editor-in-chief of *Tehelka*, praying for initiation of suo-moto contempt proceedings against the respondents. The application of Amicus Curiae drew the attention of the Supreme Court to the scandalous statement made by Respondent No.1, Prashant Bhushan, and published in the issue of *Tehelka* magazine dated 5 September 2009. Thus an important contempt case started, and I thought this gave the people an opportunity to raise the important issue of judicial corruption before the highest court. I, therefore, made an application in the contempt case against Prashant Bhushan and Tarun Tejpal to be impleaded as Respondent No.3. In the application, I stated that there was a time when it was almost impossible to even think that a judge of a High Court or the Supreme Court could be corrupt, but now the situation had changed. In fact in March 2010, a sitting Chief Justice of Gujarat High Court said that 20 per cent of the judges are corrupt. I further stated that I completely stand by Prashant Bhushan when he says that the eight of the last sixteen CJIs had been corrupt and that in fact two of them had personally told the applicant while they were in office that their immediate predecessor and immediate successor were corrupt judges. The names of these four are included in the list of the eight corrupt CJIs. I requested the Supreme Court to make me a party to this contempt case so that I am also suitably punished for it. I said that it would be a great honour to spend time in jail for making an effort to achieve an honest and clean judiciary for the people of India.

As my application was proceeding in the court, it became a public document and, therefore, the press freely referred to it. In *The Times of India*, Dhananjay Mahapatra published his report with a heading in bold lettering: 'Eight chief justices were corrupt: Ex-law minister'. He also said in the subheading: 'Dares SC to Jail Him for Contempt'. Even veteran journalist Khushwant Singh took note and wrote an article in *The Tribune* on 2 October 2010 with the heading 'Judiciary and Corruption', in which he said that because of corruption in the judiciary the aam aadmi would be the ultimate loser.

Prashant Bhushan had filed his detailed counter affidavit in the contempt case in which he justified his statement that about half of the former CJIs had been corrupt. In the affidavit, Prashant said that nowhere did he accuse Justice Kapadia of being corrupt and the only issue was of judicial impropriety as Justice Kapadia heard and passed an order in favour of the company of which he himself was a shareholder. Moreover, the only counsel who could have objected and who had an adverse interest to Vedanta in the matter was Mr Sanjay Parekh who was appearing in a connected writ petition on behalf of the tribals. However, he was not permitted to even argue his case and was told in no uncertain terms that he would not be heard, since the amicus was good enough to represent the tribals. All the other counsels present i.e. of Vedanta, Orissa Mining Corporation (which was in partnership with Vedanta for the mining), State of Orissa (which had granted the lease), and the Ministry of Environment and Forest (which had granted environmental clearance for the project) had a common interest. Moreover, the senior amicus in this case, Mr Harish Salve, already had a retainer from Vedanta and it was left to Mr Uday Lalit, the junior amicus (and now a judge in the Supreme Court), to object or not to object to Justice Kapadia's continuing to hear the case. The fact that Mr Uday Lalit did not object in no way excuses Justice Kapadia's non recusal in the matter. It is well-settled in India as well as internationally that any judge who has the slightest pecuniary interest in a case must automatically recuse himself from hearing it. Shareholding in a company, particularly in a case where the order would have enormous impact on the financial status and thus share values of that company as in the case of Vedanta/ Sterlite, is certainly a pecuniary interest. In Manak Chand vs Dr Prem Chand,[2] the Supreme Court held that, 'It is obvious that pecuniary interest, however small it may be in the subject matter of the proceedings, would wholly disqualify a member from acting as a judge.' Prashant concluded by saying that in these circumstances, his comment on Justice Kapadia's role in the Vedanta/Sterlite matter is a legitimate opinion which he is entitled to express.

When the matters were subsequently heard by the bench, it wanted me to express regret for the condemners so that they could just dispose of the petition. I, however, made it quite clear to the court in no uncertain terms that there could be no question of regret or apology and I was quite prepared to go to jail. None of what I have done amounted to contempt, but it was necessary in the overall public interest.

I had not the least doubt that if the Supreme Court sent me to jail, even for a single day, like Arundhati Roy was, the whole country would have stood by me because the people have been suffering from judicial corruption and are well-aware of its magnitude in our courts. It seems that the bench felt that discretion was the better part of valour and adjourned the court without making any orders. This is how the case has stood for the last few years. However, this entire episode raised a serious public debate in the country as to how the corruption in general and corruption in the judiciary in particular needed to be tackled.

---

[2](AIR 1957 SC 425)

3

APPOINTMENTS TO THE HIGHER JUDICIARY

Right from 1950 to 1973, although the power to appoint judges was with the executive and the role of the judiciary was only to be consulted through the Chief Justice of India assisted by the chief justices of the High Courts, the government during this period went by the advice received from the CJI without any attempt to influence his views.

It was the wafer-thin majority judgement of the Kesavananda Bharati in 1973 that led to the departure from the long-held tradition of going by the recommendation of the Chief Justice. The government, incensed by the majority judgement of Kesavananda Bharati, decided to supersede not one or two but all the three judges (Justices Shelat, Hegde, and Grover) who had decided the case against the government. The government appointed Justice Ajit Nath Ray as the next CJI, bypassing the three senior judges above him in rank because they had decided against the government, and after them A.N. Ray was the seniormost judge who had sided with the government.

This supersession was intended to send a clear signal to the judiciary that an important judgement against the executive would jeopardize the future of those judges.

The supersession which had taken place in April 1973 was

followed by the Emergency in June 1975 and the suspension of fundamental rights of life and liberty. This ultimately led to the ADM Jabalpur case; and the Supreme Court with a majority of four to one held that the right to challenge illegal detention had vanished with the suspension of fundamental rights during that period. Those imprisoned during the Emergency had no hope of being released and that included nearly all the Opposition leaders including Arun Jaitley, the current finance minister.

It was in this backdrop that the next CJI was to be selected during the Janata Party government's tenure while I was the law minister. Those who had suffered during the Emergency for their political beliefs were dead against the elevation of the two remaining senior-most judges who had sided with the government in the ADM Jabalpur case. These judges were perceived by them as having surrendered before the government for preserving their career prospects. How could they be elevated to the post of the CJI when they were responsible for the sufferings of lakhs of people on account of their judgement which was seen as motivated? At that point, Jayaprakash Narayan, the conscience-keeper of the Janata government, requested me to consider this factor while deciding on the appointment of the next CJI.

In spite of the pressure from different sources, I chose to go by the mandate of the Constitution by widening the consultation to all the judges of the Supreme Court and the chief justices of all the High Courts. There was near unanimity among the judges that the principle of seniority in the selection of the chief justice should be restored. As the question as to who appoints the judges has a great impact on the independence of the judiciary, we decided to follow the advice of the judiciary, in spite of reluctance from many of my colleagues in the government, to preserve and maintain the independence of the judiciary in all its majesty which we regarded as an integral part of the basic features of the Constitution.

I am glad that this was accepted and the government agreed to the elevation of Justice Chandrachud as the next CJI and by implication also the elevation of Justice Bhagwati as his successor. As law minister in the Janata Party Government from 1977 to 1979, I can say with authority that each and every appointment was made strictly according to the recommendations of the CJI without the slightest attempt to influence his views.

I recently read an opinion of Mr Arun Jaitley where he has referred to this failure of the Supreme Court during the Emergency as an example of its fallibility. However, one should remember that it was the direct result of the political class meddling with the appointment process from 1973 onwards. In fact the period of the Emergency demonstrates the dangers of the executive having the last word in the appointment of judges to the higher judiciary.

From 1980 onwards, after the Janata Party regime ended, the executive again started interfering in the selection of judges and thus the course correction during the Janata government was short-lived. As political attempts to influence the views of the CJs in the High Courts as also the CJI increased, the need to correct the situation was felt in the Supreme Court leading to the collegium[3] judgements.

The Constitution provides for a council of ministers to simply 'aid and advise' the President of India. It does not say that the advice is binding on the President. In fact this issue was raised by Dr Rajendra Prasad, the first president of India, soon after the Constitution came into force. The Attorney General M.C. Setalvad opined that notwithstanding the language used, the President was bound by the advice of the council of ministers.

---

[3] Invented by the Supreme Court of India in the Second Judges Case (Supreme Court Advocates-on-Record Association vs Union of India) 1993.

This view was also endorsed by the Supreme Court in its seven-judge judgement in Shamsher Singh's case. If the advice of the council of ministers is deemed to be binding on the President, then why wouldn't the advice of the collegium be binding on the President in the same manner!

In my view therefore, consultation must mean going by the advice of the Chief Justice of India.

Can a litigant select a judge to decide his own case? If not, how can the government, actions of which are judged by the judiciary, be given a direct role in the selection of judges? Their role should be confined to giving important and useful inputs to the judiciary about the persons under the consideration of the collegium.

I am one of those who strongly believe that it is possible to appoint honest, knowledgeable, able, and objective judges capable of rendering much quicker justice through a more robust, transparent, and consultative collegium system. All shortcomings of this system can be removed by the Supreme Court itself.

It is gratifying to note that the NJAC judgement itself accepts the shortcomings of the collegium system and that the Supreme Court is having more hearings to improve the system.

In fact I have had a lot of discussions with Prashant on this question and he strongly believes that the answer lies in a full-time National Judicial Appointment Commission, which would be independent of the government as well as the judiciary and which would have credibility in the system of appointment to the higher judiciary.

According to Prashant, the collegium system has many issues such as nepotism, favouritism, arbitrariness, and opacity. In fact Justice J.S. Verma who was the chief architect of the collegium system through his judgement in the Second Judges Case has said that the system requires a reconsideration. And the alternative in the form of the National Judicial Appointment Commission (NJAC), as introduced by the BJP government in 2015, would give the government very strong powers to appoint pliant judges. The NJAC Act provided for a selection committee of six people, which included three senior-most sitting judges of the Supreme Court, the law minister, and two eminent persons to be nominated by the PM, CJI and leader of Opposition in the Lok Sabha. It also provided that the secretariat of the Appointments Commission would be in the Law Ministry. It further states that any two members of the NJAC could veto the recommendation of the other four. And experience has shown that the prime minister and the leader of the Opposition are usually in agreement about appointing weak and pliable people to regulatory institutions and those who select members of such institutions, in order to weaken regulation of the political class. There was thus justified apprehension that the NJAC would dilute independence of the judiciary by giving the government a significant say in appointments. Therefore, the Supreme Court struck down the constitutional validity of the amendment introducing the NJAC Act on the ground that it diluted the independence of the judiciary which was part of the basic structure of the Constitution.

However, the Supreme Court did not take up this opportunity to lay down any system of transparency in the selection of judges. On the other hand, it left it to the government to devise a memorandum of procedure for selecting judges, which would have to be approved by the Chief Justice of India. This has resulted in the government trying to introduce clauses that could enable it to veto any recommendation on national security considerations. The memorandum of procedure is therefore stuck, with no agreement in sight between the government and the Chief Justice of India. The government is using this to delay appointments recommended by the collegium. Judicial appointments have thus become hostage to the battle between the government and the judiciary on who should control appointments.

The solution to this imbroglio, Prashant feels, lies in the creation of a full-time (not ex officio) body, which is independent of the government and the judiciary both and which goes about the selection in a rational and transparent manner. The business of selecting hundreds of judges in a year to the higher judiciary, if done properly, would require at least a thousand candidates to be considered and comparatively evaluated over multidimensional criteria in a fair and rational manner. This would require a full-time body, which could devote itself to this process, with a large secretariat. The job cannot be done by an ex officio body of judges and the law minister, who are extremely busy persons.

As per Prashant, there also needs to be some transparency in the selection to prevent arbitrariness or nepotism. Minimum transparency would require that the criteria for selection of judges be made known, the comparative evaluation of candidates also be made known, and names of shortlisted/selected candidates announced before appointment, so that those who have relevant information about the candidate can send it to the appointing authority. Basic criteria to judge the competence of a candidate should include integrity, competence, judicial temperament, common sense and sensitivity towards the problems of the common man, among others. A system modelled on the Judicial Appointments Commission in Britain, which follows a method to evaluate candidates based on predetermined and set criteria, is well worth considering. And the members of the selection authority could be retired judges or even laypersons and should be selected by a broad-based selection committee in which the government and the judiciary play a role, but not a dominant one. It is only such an independent full-time body that can be expected to select judges in a fair and rational manner.

I hope that in times to come, steps will be taken to have a full-time National Judicial Commission which will search for the keenest legal minds all over the country—irrespective of their age or seniority—to man the higher judiciary so that the citizens feel proud of their own judiciary. In my opinion, it is the excessive reliance on seniority and age that has played a significant part in having a considerable number of mediocre people in the higher judiciary.

4

THE MULAYAM SINGH YADAV AND AMAR SINGH CASE OF FAKE CD

Even before the first meeting of the Joint Drafting Committee for the Jan Lokpal Bill was held, the government nominees in it made a sinister move in an attempt to get rid of me from the meeting. On the evening of 13 April 2011, a CD was distributed to all media houses in Delhi which purported to show a conversation between myself, Amar Singh, and Mulayam Singh Yadav on phone. The CD presented as if I was with Amar Singh at his house and after chatting with me, he rang up Mulayam Singh Yadav to talk to me. The worst part of it was the supposed conversation between Mulayam Singh Yadav and myself in which I was telling him that as far as his case was concerned, my son, Prashant, who had excellent relations with Justice Singhvi, could successfully handle it for ₹4 crore. The suggestion clearly was that Mulayam Singh Yadav should pay the said amount to Prashant, which he would then use to bribe Justice Singhvi of the Supreme Court and get the case decided in Mulayam Singh Yadav's favour.

Amar Singh was clearly party to the conspiracy to get this fake CD made at the insistence of some of the Cabinet ministers of the Congress Party who were members of the Drafting

Committee. The CD had two objectives: Firstly, this was the time when Justice Singhvi was dealing with the 2G scam case in which some ministers of the Central Government were important accused persons. He was also dealing with another case of Amar Singh's tapes. The agenda was to make people believe the content of that CD, and subsequently affect the credibility of the Joint Drafting Committee and have Anna Hazare ask Prashant and I to resign from it. The second objective was that Justice Singhvi might feel embarrassed in continuing to hear the 2G case and that of Amar Singh's tapes.

It was on the night of 13 April when I was returning from a dinner that I got a call from a reporter of *The Indian Express* to enquire about the CD. He wanted to confirm whether the voice of the speaker in the CD was mine or not. I asked him to reach my residence after half an hour. He arrived with the CD and played it—to my utter surprise, I found that the voice on the CD sounded exactly like mine. Of course, I knew that the CD was fake but the likeness of the voice on the CD to mine left me shocked. I was confident that those who knew me would not fall for it, but was worried that the general public might be beguiled and believe that it was me on the CD.

My grandsons, Prashant's sons—Manav, Sumant, and Pawan, were also worried upon hearing it. They, along with one of the juniors of Prashant, started looking for a voice expert to ascertain the authenticity of this CD. On googling it, they found that the best voice expert was one George Papcun who lived in Santa Fe, California. So, my grandsons prepared an audio clip and transmitted it to George Papcun with the request to examine it and send a report as soon as possible. After finding out his fees, my grandsons woke me up to take my approval to remit this amount to him. I immediately agreed and the amount was remitted to him straightaway. He has a PhD in linguistics and acoustic phonetics from University of California, Los Angeles and has served as an expert witness in many famous legal cases such as the Rodney King trial and the OJ Simpson trial. He has been a consultant for the CIA, NSA, and the Secret Service.

On 16 April 2011, Papcun sent a report stating that the recording was not an authentic and valid representation of an original conversation and that he had found probable time gap in the recording, though the exact length of the time gap was not possible to ascertain.

Since I knew that the CD was fake even when *The Indian Express* reporter had played it before me, the very next morning I had filed a First Information Report (FIR) at the SHO Police Station, IP Extension, New Delhi. I had mentioned in the FIR that the CD was clearly a fabricated one as I have never had any conversation with Mulayam Singh Yadav of the kind contained in the CD, and as the contents were defamatory in nature, it amounted to an offence of forgery under Section 469 IPC, which was a cognizable offence. It was also apparent that several persons were involved in the fabrication of the CD and, therefore, it was also a case of conspiracy under Section 120B IPC.

After we had received George Papcun's report on 16 April 2011, we also contacted Truth Lab, a prestigious forensic laboratory located in Hyderabad that has an office in Delhi also. Truth Lab has a very eminent advisory board chaired by the former Chief Justice of India—Justice M.N. Venkatachaliah. The lab immediately got the CD forensically examined by its experts and sent us their report on 17 April 2011 stating that the CD was not authentic.

Later on an interesting discovery happened when the Truth Lab experts were discussing the matter with me in my drawing room. They wanted the voice samples of me as well as that of Mulayam Singh Yadav and Amar Singh. I, of course, gave my sample voice. So far as Mulayam Singh and Amar Singh were concerned, it occurred to Prashant that he had filed a CD in the Supreme Court in 2006 in the case related to Amar Singh's tapes and in that CD, the voices of both of them were available. So, he immediately got hold of a copy of that CD from the file maintained in his office and handed it over to the Truth Lab experts. But before handing it over to them, my grandsons thought it wise to quickly check whether the CD had decent quality voice exemplars. What they found while playing the CD astounded us—some of the sentences spoken by Mulayam Singh Yadav in that CD from 2006 pulled from our archives were identical to the ones in the new fake CD! The full sentence identical in voice in both the CDs was: '*Ab inko kaun samjhaye, chahe woh grih mantri hon, ya koi aira gaira, inko kya samjhaya jaye.*' This sentence was absolutely the same in both the CDs, which clearly demonstrated that the disputed fake CD had been fabricated.

Therefore, when it became clear that the CD which had been circulated to tarnish my image, Prashant's image, as well as Justice Singhvi's, was fabricated, I filed a Contempt Petition in the Supreme Court enclosing the fabricated CD with the report of Dr George Papcun and that of Truth Lab of India.

In the meantime, it appears that the investigating agency, on account of the sensitive nature of the matter, had contacted the then Home Minister P. Chidambaram and he had directed for the CD to be examined by the Central Forensic Science Laboratory (CFSL) of CBI at Lodhi Road, New Delhi. They had submitted a report dated 17 April 2011 to the Additional Deputy Commissioner of Police (Crime) in which they had stated that the recorded conversation in the CD could not have been tampered with because the conversation was in continuity and no abrupt change in speech signal could be detected. And the recorded conversation was in contextual continuity, and no change in background noise pattern throughout the recording could be observed.

Curiously, this report was signed by all the four experts of the Forensic Laboratory, which is never done as the reports are signed only by a single expert who examines the CD. Perhaps, it was done with the intention of making all the experts parties to the report so that none of them may change their stand later.

We, therefore, held a press conference and played both the CDs before the reporters to clearly establish that the CD containing my purported telephonic conversation with Mulayam Singh Yadav was a fabricated one.

It appears then that the authorities, including the Home Minister, became a little nervous and, in order to shield themselves, sent the CD to CFSL, Chandigarh, which was another government laboratory, for a fresh examination. Meanwhile, I had exchanged letters with the Home Minister; and he had admitted that the CDs had been sent to both the CFSLs of the government at his instance.

I must also mention that at that time a copy of the report of the Delhi CFSL, which had found the CD to be authentic, had not been made public. However, since in the meantime, the CD had also been sent to Chandigarh CFSL, *The Indian Express* came up with a report on 4 May 2011 that the CD had evidence of 'cut and paste' and also stated that the Delhi Police Special Cell investigating the case had sent the CD to Chandigarh CFSL only last Tuesday for a second opinion. I then sent a signed letter on 4 May 2011 to L.N. Rao, ACP, Special Cell with one of my juniors asking whether the statements of Mulayam Singh Yadav and Amar Singh had been recorded as to whether they had any conversation as purportedly recorded in the CD in question, and asking for copies of that and also copies of the CDSL report. The investigating officer told my junior that he knew nothing about it. The next day, *The Times of India* also carried the same report further stating that the Chandigarh CFSL senior officials stated that the report had been submitted to the Special Cell of Delhi Police four days earlier through a special messenger. I then sent another letter to B.K. Gupta, Commissioner of Police, Delhi on 5 May 2011 asking for copies of the two reports of CFSL. However, no one in the Delhi Police was prepared to give me any information. I, therefore, sent a personal letter to Home Minister P. Chidambaram with a copy to the then Prime Minister, Manmohan Singh, on 6 May 2011 stating all the facts. It had become obvious to me that the Home Minister was clearly a party to the fabrication.

It is noteworthy that when the CFSL (CBI) Delhi gave its report that the CD was genuine, it was headed by an ad hoc director, who awaited his confirmation by the Home Ministry. He could therefore be pressurized by the Home Minister to give any kind of report.

I also addressed a letter to the Prime Minister on 9 May 2011 in which I stated that the CFSL Delhi report was signed by four experts instead of one, which was an eyebrow-raising departure from standard procedure. And that their head, Director Rajinder Singh, was at that time holding the post in ad hoc capacity and his regular appointment has to be made by the appointments committee chaired by the PM, in which the Home Minister is also a member. I concluded by saying that the CFSLs are very prestigious scientific labs in the country and if this lab could give such an absurd report, declaring an obviously fabricated CD as being authentic, no court hereafter would find it possible to rely on any forensic report of the CFSL (CBI) Delhi.

On 8 May 2011, I sent another letter to the Home Minister stating that since I had written to the ACP, Special Cell, on 4 May 2011 asking for copies of the forensic reports, I received a reply from him stating, 'I am directed to inform you that the case is at the initial stage of investigation. Divulging any document/ information to any one may hamper the investigation.' Since, however, the CFSL Delhi report had already been released, and was doing the rounds in the media, I enclosed a photocopy of that report, which was signed by, not one, but four experts and in the meantime the report of CFSL Chandigarh had been received which clearly indicated that it was a 'cut and paste' job. I further wrote in my letter that nobody is able to fathom as to why one forensic report has been released and the other is being kept in a 'DOUBLE KEY SAFE'. I mentioned that moreover, the Director of CBI, CFSL, located in Delhi, was only an ad hoc appointee to the post of Director and in order to get confirmed on this post he would ingratiate to the powers that the people of India may easily guess as to which persons are behind the smear campaign against the civil society members of the Lokpal Bill drafting committee. I concluded by saying that there is a perception in the public that perhaps an effort might be on to try to pressurize the CFSL Chandigarh to change its report, and that this is the reason to keep it under wraps for so long.

It was only thereafter that I received a reply dated 10 May 2011 from the Home Minister, along with which he enclosed the letter dated 7 May 2011 from the Assistant Commissioner of Police, L.N. Rao, addressed to me stating that it was not possible to supply me the required CFSL report as it may hamper the investigation.

Thereafter, the investigating police filed a closure report with the court as required by law stating that it was not possible to fix any guilt on any person regarding the CD.

I then filed an application before the magistrate concerned requesting that the closure report be rejected and to get this matter thoroughly investigated. The reasons for this request that I cited in the application were that there are contradictory averments from the police regarding the recording of statements of Shri Amar Singh or Shri Mulayam Singh under 161 Cr.P.C; the report from CFSL Chandigarh was not being made available and that this CD was fabricated for the purpose of trying to induce Justice G.S. Singhvi to recuse himself from the 2G Spectrum case and also the Amar Singh tape case, which were pending in his court.

It must be said to the credit of the Magistrate concerned that he read the papers in full and was satisfied that there had not been a proper investigation in the matter and he, therefore, by a detailed order, rejected the closure report and directed the police to investigate the matter further. The investigating authorities, who had so far not recorded the statements of Mulayam Singh Yadav and Amar Singh, were forced to record them, and while Mulayam Singh stated that he could not remember the matter at all and, therefore, was unable to say whether any such telephonic conversation had taken place between him and me. Amar Singh, however, stated that, while he could confirm that I had a telephonic talk with Mulayam Singh Yadav from his residence, he could not confirm as to what happened in the conversation because he claimed to have left the room when I was talking on the phone and so had not heard as to what had taken place. He clearly, therefore, wanted to avoid any responsibility in the matter. Since Amar Singh stated that I was at his residence when he made me talk to Mulayam Singh, which was not true at all, it was clear that Amar Singh was party to the fabrication of the CD.

As a proper investigation would implicate a great many important people in the preparation of the CD, the police could not submit a closure report saying that no clear evidence is available and the matter had to be closed. However, the closure report, so far, has not been accepted by the Magistrate and the matter is still pending before him. I do hope that the Magistrate will see to it that this matter is thoroughly investigated and all those who are guilty are brought to book.

5
ANNA ANDOLAN

BACKGROUND

The major cases of corruption which had come to light during the UPA-II government and which had shown the extent of corruption being beyond any limits of imagination were the following three:

1. The 2G Spectrum Scam
2. The Commonwealth Games Scam
3. The Coalgate Scam

It is necessary to understand, at least briefly, about these four events in order to appreciate why the public was so angry at the government during the 'Anna Andolan'.

1. The 2G Scam

The airways of each country belong to itself and since the IT business uses these waves in a big way, they are every nation's valuable property. In a republic country, all these valuable resources belong to the people and the government manages them for their benefit. The Constitution, therefore, mandates that the government uses these valuable resources so that the people benefit from it. The most convenient way that any part of these assets can be commercially exploited is only by transfer of that asset to private companies at the best possible prices i.e. by means of an auction.

The 2G case became sensational because valuable resources like the 2G spectrum were transferred to the companies, not at their market value, but at a much lower rate because the politicians in power then got huge kickbacks from the corporates. This makes it very easy to understand as to why there is always a fight over portfolios in a coalition government; because in select portfolios there are huge rent-seeking opportunities.

Niira Radia was a lobbyist for Mukesh Ambani and Ratan Tata with a keen interest in the allocation of ministerial portfolios. In 2007–09, the Income Tax Department, on the basis of a complaint, obtained permission from the Home Ministry to tap her phones. The tapping went on for almost 300 days. The complaint on the basis of which this tapping of the phone was done, was an anonymous letter sent to the Finance Ministry in which it was claimed that Radia was a covert operator of a foreign government. Over 5,000 conversations between Radia and all kinds of persons in powerful positions as well as several journalists were recorded.

Somebody gave copies of these audio recordings, which had been with the Income Tax Department, to Prashant. Let me state here that many whistle-blowers give documents to Prashant and they do so with full confidence that their names would never be revealed to anyone including the Supreme Court of India. Prashant applies various tests to determine whether the documents supplied to him are genuine or not and if they are of sufficient public interest and only if he is convinced that they are genuine, does he use them as material for his Public Interest cases, which he institutes mainly in the Supreme Court, and sometimes in the High Court with telling results.

On receipt of copies of the audio recordings of Niira Radia tapes, Prashant filed them in his pending case relating to 2G scam because these tapes shed some light on how A. Raja had been appointed Telecom Minister by then Prime Minister Manmohan Singh as well as certain other facts relating to the 2G scam. Once these tapes were filed in the Supreme Court, they became public documents and two magazines *Open* and *Outlook* obtained copies of these audio recordings and published transcripts of some of those in November 2010.

Niira Radia's telephone had been tapped by the Income Tax authorities from 2009 onwards and they contained very stark revelations as to how the government affairs were being run and managed. It was through these tapes that it was revealed that a judge of the Delhi High Court had taken a bribe of ₹9 crore for one single case.

In May 2007, A. Raja had become the telecom minister. He was an MP from the DMK party and at the insistence of the DMK, had been allotted the Telecom Ministry by Prime Minister Manmohan Singh. In September, the Telecom Ministry invited applications for the allotment of 2G spectrum with the deadline being 1 October 2007. The ministry received 575 applications for licences from 46 companies.

On 10 January 2008, Department of Telecommunications decided to issue licences on first-come, first-served basis advancing the cut-off date from 1 October to 25 September 2007 and announcing on its website that those applying between 3.30 p.m. and 4.30 p.m. would be granted licences in accordance with its policy. In May 2009, a complaint was filed with the Chief Vigilance Commissioner (CVC) by Arun Agarwal, a close friend of Prashant's, highlighting the low-cost spectrum being granted to Swan Telecom. The CVC directed the Central Bureau of Investigation (CBI) to investigate the case.

On 1 July 2009, the Delhi High Court ruled that the advancement of the date was illegal.

On 16 November 2009, the CBI started investigating the taped conversation of corporate lobbyist Niira Radia to learn about the involvement of middlemen in the grant of spectrum to telecom companies, and they sought sanction from the Director General (Income Tax) for investigation of Radia and her company.

On 13 March 2010, the Supreme Court upheld the Delhi High Court ruling that the advancement of the cut-off date was illegal, and on 31 March, the Comptroller and Auditor General of India (CAG) reported large scale irregularities in spectrum allocation. When the telephone conversation between A. Raja and Niira Radia, recorded by the Income Tax Department, became public, the Centre for Public Interest Litigation, through Prashant, filed a petition in the Delhi High Court for a special investigation of the scam, but on 25 May that year the Delhi High Court dismissed the petition.

On an appeal being filed in the Supreme Court by Prashant against the decision of the Delhi High Court, the Supreme Court admitted the appeal and asked the government and A. Raja to file a reply within ten days, particularly on the allegation regarding the ₹170,000-crore scam in granting telecom licences in 2008. In November, the CAG submitted a report on the 2G spectrum to the government stating that the loss of ₹176,000 crore had been caused to the exchequer by the illegal allocation of 2G spectrum.

Thus far, people had heard of bribes in hundreds, thousands, even lakhs, but to talk of the government causing a loss to the exchequer of ₹176,000 crore was a mind-boggling figure. One could imagine the anger which this revelation by the CAG could generate in the public against the government and the politicians. In December 2010, the Supreme Court decided to monitor the CBI enquiry.

The CBI is a Central Government institution. Its director and other staff are appointed by the government who are liable to be transferred and action can be taken against them by the government if such a situation arises. Therefore, they do not act independently. It is natural for a person to care for his own interest first, and then his duties. The CBI officers, therefore, could not dare to act against the ministers of the very government which exercises supervisory powers over them. This was the rationale for many of us drafting the Lokpal Bill in which care was taken that the Lokpal would enjoy total independence from any government so as to be trusted by the people for an honest investigation even against the highest and the mightiest.

In February 2011, A. Raja, his Personal Secretary R.K. Chandolia, and former Telecom Secretary Siddharth Behuria were arrested in the telecom scam. It was the first time in history when a Central Cabinet Minister had been arrested and this had become possible only because the CBI investigation was being monitored by the Supreme Court. So, it was not possible for the CBI to deviate from its obvious duty which the emerging evidence in the case under investigation dictated. Raja was finally sent to Tihar jail on 17 February 2011.

In June 2011, M.K. Kanimozhi, the daughter of DMK patriarch, late M. Karunanidhi, was also arrested for the same. This was a sensational event because Karunanidhi was a very powerful politician at the time and the UPA government could not have survived without his continuing support.

The Radia tapes disclosed a sordid story as to how the

governments were functioning under political leaders and how massive corruption was thriving and how even a personally honest Prime Minister like Manmohan Singh was condoning it due to coalition compulsions.

It was the first time that the people of the country were watching the immense power of the Supreme Court and what a PIL in the High Court or the Supreme Court could achieve, and what the revelations made by CAG could do as well. This furnished an ideal background to the success of Anna Andolan in August 2011.

2. The Commonwealth Games Scam

In the year 2010, the Commonwealth Games took place in Delhi. It was a very important event and massive infrastructural upgradation projects had been undertaken in preparation for it, although understandably many, including Mani Shankar Aiyyar from the Congress Party, objected to such profligacy when a large section of our population is still living in abject poverty. The point, however, is that with such massive spending came an even more massive corruption opportunity.

In July 2010, the CVC released a report showing irregularities in up to fourteen Commonwealth Games projects. Irregularities such as work orders had been awarded at higher prices to ineligible agencies. It was also found that simple things such as toilet paper rolls valued at US$2 had in fact cost US$80, mirrors worth US$98 had cost US$220 and Altitude Training Simulators worth US$11,830 had cost US$250,190—about twenty times their original cost.

The day after the conclusion of the Games, the government announced the formation of a sub-committee to probe the allegations of corruption and mismanagement against the

Organizing Committee. The probe committee was led by former CAG V.K. Shunglu. On 25 April 2011, the CBI arrested former Commonwealth Games Organizing Committee Chairman—Suresh Kalmadi—under Section 120B (criminal conspiracy) and Section 420 (cheating) of the Indian Penal Code, 1860 and on 20 May 2011, CBI filed its first charge sheet in a Special CBI Court against Kalmadi. In the charge sheet, it was alleged that Kalmadi was the main accused in awarding Timing, Scoring and Result (TSR) System contract to a Swiss firm. The CBI also named two companies and eight other persons including former Secretary General, Lalit Bhanot, and former Director General, V.K. Verma, of the CWG Organizing Committee. Apart from criminal conspiracy, they were also charged with forging documents and presenting them as genuine under the Prevention of Corruption Act.

3. Coalgate Scam

Mining of coal was authorized to be carried out only by the government's Coal India Limited. During the UPA regime, the government decided to allocate 194 coal blocks to public and private enterprises in an ad hoc manner between 2004 and 2009. As it is the CAG who audits the functioning of the government and the exercise of its powers, it initially estimated the loss caused to the exchequer to be ₹10.6 lakh crore, but it was scaled down in the final report tabled in the Parliament to ₹1.86 lakh crore.

Now, an amount of nearly ₹2 lakh crore is bound to baffle the public imagination. The report created great waves and thus became an integral part of the public's frustration with the politicians.

As the coal stocks are very valuable assets of the nation

they cannot be gifted away to private companies for a song and without the overriding public interest in mind. The allocation of these coal blocks should clearly have been done through a public auction. It had also become evident that the allocations had been made when former Prime Minister Dr Manmohan Singh was heading the Coal Ministry.

On the basis of the CAG report, a Public Interest Litigation was filed in the Supreme Court and ultimately the CBI had to initiate a probe into the alleged corruption in the allocation of coal blocks. The former Coal Secretary, P.C. Parekh, who was charged by CBI in the Coalgate Scam, had hit out at Dr Manmohan Singh for overruling his call for auctions and for continuing arbitrary allotment of coal blocks. Finally, the Supreme Court came out with the verdict that the allocations were to be cancelled and directed that they be disposed of by means of public auctions or by inviting tenders in public interest. A large number of prosecutions have also been launched in the Coalgate scam by the CBI.

◆

These were the major scams which were highlighted by Team Anna during the Anna Andolan and it had been pointed out that it was only due to the Supreme Court that the offenders in these scams could be brought to book. But since the Supreme Court cannot possibly deal with such a large number of cases of corruption and monitor their investigation, it was necessary to have an institution which would be independent of the government and investigate the matters without fear or favour.

I remember having heard that during the period when M.G. Ramachandran (MGR) was the chief minister of Tamil Nadu and Karunanidhi was the leader of the Opposition, the main source of corruption in that was liquor—which was in the

State List and, therefore, its State Government had full powers to deal with it. As is well-known, the excise duty on liquor is very high compared to the cost of manufacture of liquor; and for the possibility of selling bottles without the payment of excise duty any seller would be willing to pay a huge bribe to the chief minister of the State. I was told that when any liquor baron would go to then Chief Minister MGR with the bribe, the first question that the latter would ask was whether the baron had paid a share to the leader of the Opposition, namely Karunanidhi. The share of the leader of the Opposition was about 15 per cent, so that 85 per cent would come to the ruling party. This was a convenient arrangement so that the Opposition does not raise a hue and cry about the continuing corruption in the liquor trade.

◆

Kisan Baburao 'Anna' Hazare

In April and August 2011, a wave took over India—the likes of which had never happened before either in India or in any other country. It was an event that had been watched by the whole country on their TV sets and had electrified the people. This was the Anna Andolan (movement) which had two phases: first from 4–9 April 2011; and the second took place in August 2011 which lasted almost two weeks.

Both the phases of the Andolan centred around Anna's hunger strike—in April at Jantar Mantar and in August at the Ramlila Maidan, New Delhi. Kisan Baburao Hazare is a former Army man, who did not occupy any high position in the Army's hierarchy. Post his retirement, he had settled down in his village Ralegan Siddhi in Maharashtra. He has modelled himself on

Gandhian principles—upholding non-violence and believing in the pursuit of truth. He lives with limited means in a temple and even dresses in a simple way—in a white kurta and dhoti and a white Gandhi cap. He is known to believe in non-violent ways, particularly resorting to fast unto death to achieve his public objective.

Anna may not be highly educated, but he possesses great common sense, speaks lucidly, and mesmerizes his audience with his simplicity and Gandhian ways.

He has a long record of struggle against corruption in Maharashtra by launching his fast unto death, which is called his 'anshan'. One of his first such anshans was way back in 1991 when he launched the 'Bhrashtachar Virodhi Jan Aandolan' and subsequently went on a hunger strike in Alandi, Maharashtra. As a consequence of this campaign, six ministers had to resign and 400 officers were removed. Since his battles have always been for a common cause, they leave a very deep impression on the people and that has been at the root of his success in various fights in Maharashtra. He has created a large following in every nook and corner of that State.

He also helped develop his village by properly utilizing the resources offered by various government schemes and ensured that not a single rupee of those funds was misused or misappropriated by anybody. By undertaking projects such as check bunds and water reservoirs, he has totally altered the economy of his village and people who had left for the cities are now returning to it. He insists there is no alcohol or tobacco consumption in the village, the schools are managed locally and well. We saw all these achievements when one of the meetings of the Core Committee of Anna Team was fixed in Ralegan Siddhi. His village is now prosperous and being emulated by the nearby ones. The success of Anna Andolan was in no small measure due to the personality of Anna Hazare—his simplicity, honesty, his devotion to causes dear to him and his readiness to even sacrifice his life for those causes. When he came to the notice of lakhs of people in Delhi for the first time in 2011 and by millions of others through media coverage, they instinctively felt that they were watching Mahatma Gandhi in a new incarnation.

Before 2011, Anna's work was confined to the State of Maharashtra, and while he might have been reasonably well-known in Maharashtra, hardly anybody knew him outside of it up until April 2011. That was when he sat on a fast unto death at Jantar Mantar in New Delhi and within a couple of days he became a cult-like figure in India.

Anna Andolan of 2011 was indeed a phenomenon, the like of which had not been witnessed anywhere in the world before. Its ultimate aim was the passing of a law enacting the formation of strong Lokpal (anti-corruption ombudsman). However, that aim was not fully achieved as the Lokpal Act passed by the UPA-II was not as strong as we had hoped for. The real success of Anna Andolan was the fact that for the first time the people of India realized that they have the power to get laws made through mass action.

Earlier, people questioned the quality of governance once in every five years only; now they are prompted to discuss the merits and demerits of every single important action of the government on a day-to-day basis. This is the reason we have organized debates on all measures which are under the consideration of the legislatures or the executive on many news channels today. The effect of this is that every government and its functionaries have to be on their toes all the time because all their acts are being scrutinized and debated by 'we the people'.

As I was one of the important participants in the Anna

Movement, I have decided to write this first-hand account of the movement, its objectives, and how it created momentum.

It is now well-known that from 2009–10 several major scams made corruption a major issue in the country. People started believing that their miseries were on account of the pervasive corruption in the entire country. Politics, which at the time of freedom movement and even during the early years after India secured its freedom, was regarded a matter of public service and the politicians evoked respect and reverence among the people; but things had started deteriorating in the decades that followed. In 2009 and 2010, some cases taken up by the Supreme Court, for which it adopted a new approach, resulted in the successful investigation of various scams like the 2G, Coalgate, and Commonwealth Games ones. Some Central ministers even went to jail for it. However, this activist-like approach of the Supreme Court was not enough because the institution could not possibly have enough time to unearth all the scams in the country. The people, therefore, started wondering whether there could be some other way which would be able to tackle corruption. Even judicial corruption had come to the fore and, therefore, people felt that judiciary alone could not be relied upon for ridding the country of the corruption menace.

In August 2010, some of us—Santosh Hegde, Nikhil Dey, Prashant, Shekhar Singh, J.M. Lyngdoh, and myself—met at India International Centre and prepared the first draft of the Lokpal Bill. The main idea of the Bill was to create an investigative agency which will not be under the control of the politicians. It is well-known that while the police is under the control of the State Governments, which means under the ruling politicians of the States, the CBI is under the control of the Central Government, which means under politicians at the

Centre. They are able to abuse their positions to make huge amounts of money, which apart from going into the pockets of politicians and bureaucrats also goes to political party funding for elections campaigns as well as for the day-to-day functioning of those parties.

The idea of Lokpal Bill, therefore, was to create a new institution called Lokpal with full powers for investigation in all cases of corruption and to be answerable only to the people of India and not to any political bosses. The Bill contemplated that a Selection Committee to select the chairperson and the members of Lokpal institution would be created not by the government but be an independent body comprising the Prime Minister, the Leader of Opposition in the Lok Sabha, two judges of the Supreme Court and two Chief Justices of High Courts, to be selected by the collegium of all Supreme Court judges, as well as the Chief Election Commissioner and the Comptroller and Auditor General of India. As the government would not have any hand in the constitution of the Selection Committee, it would not be in a position to influence the functioning of the Lokpal, the members of which were to be selected by such a Selection Committee. In order to ensure that the Lokpal institution itself did not become corrupt, a provision was included which gave a right to any individual to approach the Supreme Court against any member and the court was given the authority to remove any corrupt member. There was also a provision for a statutory protection to 'whistle-blowers'— those, part of an organization, who have considerable inside information and who are prepared to expose corrupt people. Such whistle-blowers, being in the government, are penalized by their political masters. It was for this very reason that it was contemplated that they must have full protection against such victimization.

It was also provided in the Bill to fix time limits within which such routine matters were required to be disposed of—like a ration card, a driving licence, a building permit, and other such things. The idea was that some statutory authority in the Lokpal institution will fix time limits for the performance of these routine duties and will have the power to penalize individual officers who were found derelict in performing their duties. The Bill, therefore, contained many essential provisions to effectively deal with the growing menace of corruption in the country. Evidently, such a Bill did not suit the politicians because politics for them will cease to be a profitable vocation.

It is my firm belief that political offices should be occupied only by those people who have a burning desire to serve society without indulging in any corruption. It is also my long-held belief that the main function of politicians and political parties is to identify the problems of different sections of society to consider what best possible solutions could be with the help of experts. And also that all such campaigns, in order to be effective, have to be peaceful.

I have no doubt that if the Lokpal Bill drafted by us had been enacted, it would have ushered in a totally different type of politics in the country. I know from my long experience that if a political party helps different sections of society by its acts, there are plenty of people who are prepared to financially support such a party.

After the Lokpal Bill had been drafted, it was decided to have a public meeting at Ramlila Maidan on 30 January 2011—which was also the day of Mahatma Gandhi's death anniversary. Baba Ramdev and Sri Sri Ravi Shankar brought a large number of people in their own buses for this public meeting. They must have had their own reasons for that—which was probably to take advantage of the movement that was being launched. Even though the organizers did not expect such a huge response, it transpired that the gathering of about 25,000 people was beyond their expectations.

When I addressed the gathering on that occasion I spoke about how looking at the vast multitude of people that had come, I was reminded of another historic occasion at that very Ramlila Maidan when in June 1975 Jayaprakash Narayan had addressed a huge audience to ask for Mrs Indira Gandhi's resignation after the Allahabad High Court's verdict against her and the Supreme Court's refusal to grant her an unconditional stay order. That meeting, in due course, even though it had resulted in the proclamation of the Emergency and the detention of a large number of leaders and people, ultimately resulted in a historic election in March 1977 in which the ruling party of Mrs Gandhi was able to win only one parliamentary seat out of about 350 in North India. Looking at the enthusiasm of the people assembled, that day I could feel that the same spirit was returning and the corrupt government of Prime Minister Manmohan Singh would not be able to withstand this peaceful onslaught of the people. It does seem indeed that what I had said on 30 January 2010 at the historic Ramlila Maidan turned out to be true and there was a massive defeat of the ruling Congress Party in the next parliamentary election, although it took place several years later.

It was Arvind Kejriwal, thereafter, who decided to involve Anna in the movement for the Lokpal Bill as he was known to be a valiant Gandhian crusader against corruption in Maharashtra though he was not that well-known across the rest of the country. Upon joining the movement, Anna wrote letters to the Prime Minister several times but the latter did not respond to them. Anna, therefore, sent an ultimatum to the Prime Minister stating that a Lokpal Bill should be drafted by a joint team of the government and civil society members who fight against corruption and if he did not take the required decision, Anna would sit on a fast unto death in Delhi. It was then that the Prime Minister called him for a discussion on the 7 March 2011. Some of us went with Anna to meet the Prime Minister at 7, Race Course Road—his official residence. Incidentally, it was the same house in which I had lived for three years from 1977 to 1980 as the Law Minister in Morarji Desai's Janata Dal government. The meeting, however, was not very satisfactory. Therefore, we, the civil society members, made it known that Anna would go ahead with his fast.

◆

April Phase

It was at this stage that some technical experts who were supporting the movement advised us to use the social media to spread the message of the Anna Movement. This was indeed a very important step by which news of the movement reached all corners of India in a moment. The mobile revolution in no small measure played a very significant role and greatly contributed to the success we achieved.

Team Anna decided that Anna should begin his Anshan on 5 April 2011 at Jantar Mantar where a big stage was put up and was equipped with loud speakers and various pictures with the objective of creating a national fever in favour of the movement. The National Flag was freely used not only by the organizers, but also by the people who were participating in the movement. It was also decided that participating in the movement could be symbolized by wearing Gandhi caps with the words '*Main Anna Hun*' (I am Anna) on it, so that each participant could identify with the simple Gandhian Anna.

As the fast was to begin on 5 April, Anna had planned to come to Delhi from Ralegaon Siddhi on the 4 April and was to stay at Kiran Bedi's house in Uday Park. As the media had begun covering Anna's movements, the people in Delhi came to know about his impending arrival in Delhi and a vast multitude of people reached the airport. Anna's journey from there to Kiran Bedi's house itself became a big rally which was shown on most news channels.

A staunch Gandhian, the first thing Anna wanted to do on his arrival was to visit Raj Ghat to pay his respects to Father of the Nation and to seek his blessings. So, on the morning of 5 April, before beginning his fast, he first proceeded to visit Raj Ghat. There was a massive crowd awaiting him there as well. Anna Hazare has a great presence, and his devotion to Gandhi and his principles has always been evident. His very appearance creates a deep impression on people, which is why his audience instinctively developed reverence for that old man dressed in simple clothes.

For political rallies, people are brought to the venue not only by hired buses, but they are also paid some money to compensate against their loss of wages for the day. They are also given a sumptuous meal and they treat the political rally as a paid picnic. However, the crowd in the Anna Movement was completely different. They reached the venue on their own, spent their own money, losing their own wages—but all due to their strong belief that an emissary from God was coming to free them from various corrupt agencies—the corrupt police, the corrupt judiciary, the corrupt bureaucracy and, above all, the corrupt politicians.

As soon as the fast began at Jantar Mantar on 5 April, some politicians of the opposition parties tried to take advantage of the movement to target the ruling party—the Congress. Sharad Yadav, who was the president of the Janata Dal (U) and who had also been a part of the JP Movement, also reached Jantar Mantar that day and wanted to make a speech. The assembled protesters, however, raised a storm and prevented him from speaking. The action of the assembled crowd demonstrated the hatred of the people in general against the political class and not merely against the ruling party. The same thing happened with Uma Bharati and Ram Jethmalani as well—in fact in their case the crowd did not even allow them to reach the dais.

It was on that stage that Anna spoke the words which impressed in people's minds the true spirit of a republic: '*Janata to malik hai aur neta log unka naukar hai. Lekin naukar log apne ko malik maan gaye hai aur malik jaisa bartav asli malik—janta— ke sath karte hain.*' Roughly translated, it means that the public is the master and the minister is the servant; but nowadays the minister thinks he is the master and the public is the servant. One can imagine the proud feeling even a poor rickshawallah had on hearing these words that he was a 'malik' and every minister, including the prime minister, was his paid servant. This, to a great extent, altered the equation between the people and the government and their acts of governance.

Thanks to the support from the media especially the news channels, the message of the movement was spreading all over India like wild fire and similar protests were being organized by people in different places. On the evening of 6 April, people organized a candlelight march at India Gate in support of the Anna Andolan. It seemed that people felt they were at the threshold of a revolution and were keen to participate in it.

As the movement gained strength all over India by leaps and bounds, the government started to get nervous and wanted to find channels of communication with the leaders of the movement. Although the government had earlier said that a Drafting Committee in which the Manmohan Singh government had participated would be unconstitutional, they changed their stand later and indicated that they were prepared to have a Joint Drafting Committee for the Lokpal Bill. However, while Team Anna insisted that it should be constituted by a government notification, the government's position was that it would be a constitutional impropriety to do so and they were not prepared to issue a notification.

By 8 April the situation had become too hot for the government and they finally agreed to have a Joint Drafting Committee with five ministers and five nominees of Anna. It was Kapil Sibal who was the face of the negotiating team from the government's side, and I was told that the five names sent to him from Team Anna were: Anna Hazare, Justice Santosh Hegde, Prashant Bhushan, Arvind Kejriwal, and myself. Kapil Sibal had no objection to the first four names, but was not happy with mine. I was told that when my name was mentioned, he put down his pen and asked if they could suggest somebody else in my place. This was, however, not acceptable to the emissaries of Team Anna. It is my conjecture that the reason for Kapil Sibal's objection to my name could only be one—his belief that during the negotiations among the members of the Drafting Committee while they could hoodwink every other member, it would not be possible to do the same with me because of my knowledge and experience in constitutional law.

The government also indicated that a notification would be issued the next morning constituting the Joint Drafting Committee of which Shri Pranab Mukherjee would be the chairman and I the co-chairman.

By the time that final breakthrough came late on the evening of 8 April, the situation in various parts of the country had become very tense and there was the danger of people losing their patience and indulging in violence. Arvind argued that since the notification would come only on the morning of 9 April, it would not be proper to share the breakthrough with the people of the country on the night of 8th. When I came to know of this, I reached he venue of the anshan and went up the dais, spoke to Anna and told him clearly that the news must be shared with the people of the country so that the danger of any violence anywhere could be avoided. It was then decided that a meeting would be held at the residence of Swami Agnivesh which was very close to the venue of the anshan—in the Jantar Mantar complex itself; and all the important members of Team Anna including Prashant, Arvind Kejriwal, Manish Sisodia, Kiran Bedi, and myself would meet there. I decided to use a trump card to overcome the objection of those who wanted the announcement to be postponed till the next morning, by telling them clearly that if my proposal to make an announcement straightaway was not accepted, I would denounce the movement and dissociate myself from it. The dissenters were left with no option and everyone accepted the suggestion. So, Anna and I came back to the dais. I took the mike and announced that I had some very good news for the people of India: The government had agreed to Anna's demands and the following morning a notification would be issued announcing the appointment of a Joint Drafting Committee of which a government nominee would be the chairman and an Anna nominee would be the co-chairman. But since Anna never breaks his fast at night, but only in the morning, the fast would be broken the next day. I added that victory has been achieved and everyone should start celebrating. As soon as this was flashed on TV, news of victory celebrations began pouring in from all over the country.

This is how the first phase of the Anna Andolan came to an end.

◆

The Inside Story of the Joint Drafting Committee

A state-of-the-art conference hall was readied in room no.41 of North Block for the deliberations of the Joint Drafting Committee. On one side of the table sat the government nominees—Finance Minister Pranab Mukherjee as the chairman, Home Minister P. Chidambaram, Law and Justice Minister Dr Veerappa Moily, Human Resource Development Minister Kapil Sibal, and Water Resources and Minority Affairs Minister Salman Khurshid. On the other side sat the five members of the civil society with me as co-chairperson of the Drafting Committee, along with Anna Hazare, Justice Santosh Hegde, Arvind Kejriwal, and Prashant. There were also arrangements for audio recording of the proceedings along with a large number of persons present as support staff.

The Joint Drafting Committee held nine meetings in total. The first meeting was held on Saturday, 16 April 2011 at 11.30 a.m.; and the last on Tuesday, 21 June 2011 at 4.30 p.m. As all the ministers were busy people, it was understandable that they could not give early dates for the meetings and it was over a period of more than two months that these nine meetings took place. Although we, on behalf of the civil society, were keen on more meetings and with fewer intervals, we could appreciate the difficulties of the five ministers.

We also pressed for the proceedings to be video-recorded so that the people could know as to how the members of the Drafting Committee were going about the job. We gave the example of the proceedings in the two Houses of Parliament being live telecast for the benefit of the people of the country so that they could directly hear and see as to how their representatives were functioning in the two Houses. However, it seemed that the government was adamant on this issue and did not want the proceedings to be video-recorded and said that audio recording should be enough. When we raised the point that just from the audio recording the public would not be able to recognize as to who spoke a particular sentence, the Chairperson of the Committee, Pranab Mukherjee, assured us that in the text of the audio clippings the names of the speakers would be clearly mentioned.

Now, in retrospect, it is clear that the government never had the intention of drafting a satisfactory Lokpal Bill which would provide a totally independent investigation of corruption. It appeared that the government was only forced into constituting a Joint Drafting Committee because of Anna Hazare's hunger strike, which had evoked such a spontaneous response in the entire country. The government probably thought that since public memory was short, if they could while away the time in the proceedings of the Committee without the public getting to know the full details of what was really going on, they would be able to weather the storm and come out with a weak Lokpal Bill. And this is exactly what they achieved.

In the first meeting, the Chairperson mentioned that the Joint Drafting Committee of a Bill was a unique experiment which had not been attempted before. He explained that up until then the government alone had been drafting the bills and it was the select committee, to which the Parliament referred it, which was eliciting public opinion by examining witnesses. The Chairperson stated that it was the first time that even at the drafting stage a section of society had been made a part of the process and hoped that the outcome of such an exercise would be positive. He specifically requested Anna Hazare to spell out the procedural aspects to be adopted for the drafting process as expected by his group.

Anna underscored the transparency and advocated for video recording of the proceedings and also stated that the group had already shared a comprehensive draft of the Lokpal Act and that the committee should debate only on those parts on which there is no agreement between the two sides and leave the rest be, so that time could be saved.

I thereafter expressed my views in some detail and referred to the fact that India had signed the United Nations Convention against corruption in 2005 but still had not ratified it, even though countries like Pakistan had ratified it. As for which people should be covered by the Lokpal Act, I pointed out that the UN Convention defined public officials as any person who holds a legislative, executive, administrative or judicial post. I also pointed out that the Prevention of Corruption Act also included judges in the definition of public servants. I thereafter referred to Article 6(2) of the Convention and explained how it showed that a totally independent body was the soul of the matter and thus its members must be selected with care so that people could repose faith in them. Article 13(1) of the Convention also referred to participation of society in the fight against corruption. I also explained the provisions of the civil society's draft (called the Jan Lokpal Law) provided that the role of Lokpal was only to investigate, file the charge sheet, and the trial would go on as per usual procedure. However, the Bill proposed that the investigation and the trial are completed in a time-bound manner. And it was one of the functions of the Lokpal to recommend the setting up of additional courts whose recommendations would be binding on the government so that the trial in corruption cases did not get delayed.

I further pointed out that in the Jan Lokpal Bill, there was provision for the cancellation of contracts which had been procured on the basis of corruption and also for the confiscation of assets acquired by any person by means of corruption. I also explained that the Bill contemplated the Lokpal authority to comprise a chairperson and ten members which would function through benches of two or three members. So far as the selection of the chairperson and the members of the Lokpal authority was concerned, it was entrusted to a Selection Committee which would comprise the Prime Minister, the Leader of the Opposition in the Lok Sabha, two honest judges of the Supreme Court and two chief justices from the High Courts along with the Comptroller and Auditor General and the Chief Election Commissioner. Since all these persons are busy people, it was proposed in the Bill that they would be assisted by a Search Committee to be constituted in the manner laid down in the Bill.

It was also proposed in the Bill that the Lokpal will draw a Citizens' Charter of Rights in a phased manner. This related to a time-bound delivery of certain rights to citizens, like getting a ration card, driving licence, etc., within a prescribed period. Otherwise the Lokpal had the power to punish the concerned officials for non-performance in cases of delay and in the redressal of grievances.

Thereafter, the other members of the civil society and the ministers also briefly expressed their views on the procedural aspects. The Law Minister specifically stated that the government was committed to introduce the Bill in the ensuing Monsoon Session of the Parliament and, therefore, there was a period of only about sixty days to consider the Lokpal Bill in the Joint Drafting Committee (JDC).

In the next meeting of the JDC, one of the issues which came up for discussion was whether the politicians who were not elected to the legislatures but held posts within the party framework should also be covered by the Lokpal Bill. I conceded here that politicians holding party posts (even if elected from the party members) would not come under the Lokpal purview as they have not been elected by the public.

In this meeting, the then Home Minister P. Chidambram sought clarification from us regarding the applicability of Article 226 against the decisions of Lokpal. I confirmed right then that yes, the provisions of Articles 226 and 32 of the Constitution would apply and the decisions of the Lokpal would be subject to judicial review. I further clarified that even if Lokpal was set up as a constitutional authority, the decisions would still be subject to review by the Writ Courts.

The Chairperson then invited the civil society members to express their views on the Statement of Objects and Reasons which was to be made a part of the Bill. I thereupon read out the proposed Statement of Objects and Reasons from our draft of the Jan Lokpal Bill which referred to the report of N.N. Vohra Committee of 1993 relating to the nexus between criminals, police, bureaucracy, and politicians. I also referred to the various provisions in the UN Convention contained in Articles 6(2), 7(4), 8(2), 8(5), 8(6), 12, 13, and 34 being incorporated in the Statement of Objects and Reasons.

In the third meeting of the Committee, the Home Minister stated that he would be spelling out the areas of clear agreement on the principles and such areas should be eliminated from further discussions. And one of the areas that the Home Minister marked for further deliberations was the barring of the Chairperson or member of the Lokpal authority to contest elections even after ceasing to be a member of the Lokpal authority. The Home Minister also conveyed the agreement of the Committee to the selection process by a broad-based Selection Committee which should be assisted by a Search Committee. However, the composition of such Selection Committee and Search Committee, according to him, required further discussions.

The Home Minister also wanted that the consideration of complaints against the Prime Minister by the Lokpal authority should also be put in a square bracket because it required further discussions.

Justice Santosh Hegde thereupon pointed out that even in the Draft Bill formulated by the government, such a provision for covering the Prime Minister was also included. However, the Home Minister still insisted to have this issue put in a square bracket. The Home Minister also wanted a clarification as to whether the Lokpal would have the power to award punishment. I, as co-chairperson, and Justice Santosh Hegde, clarified that the Lokpal was not intended to be the judge, jury, and executioner and award of punishment would lie within the domain of only a court of competent jurisdiction.

The Home Minister also referred to clause 6(c) relating to complaint against any politician for his or her conduct inside the Parliament and indicated that the Houses of Parliament had in place the Ethics Committees and the Privileges Committees for dealing with such misconducts inside the Houses. It was clarified by me that in regard to corruption inside the Houses by any member, the Lokpal would be only making the recommendations and the decision of the Speaker or Chairman of the House would be final and such an authority could choose to disagree with the recommendations of the Lokpal.

On the matter of the Lokpal members being debarred from contesting elections, I said that the members and Chairperson should not be aspirants for any posts after completion of their tenure because if they could become candidates of any political party for any future election, it may compromise their independence while functioning as a member of the Lokpal authority. When the question was discussed as to whether judges should be excluded from the review of the Lokpal Bill, civil society members insisted that they are public servants as defined in the Prevention of Corruption Act and, hence, must be included. The Home Minister referred to the views of some other people including two former chief justices of India—Chief Justice N. Venkatachaliah and Chief Justice J.S. Verma—who were insistent that judges should not be investigated by any such Lokpal authority. He mentioned that the government side was neither for nor against any proposal on this issue and the matter would be discussed in detail at a later stage.

In the next meeting, the Home Minister raised the issue about the Lokpal being given powers of search and seizure and stated that this should be discussed later along with the issue relating to powers and jurisdiction of the Lokpal.

Another important issue discussed in that meeting related to the power of the Lokpal to authorize the tapping of telephones of any person suspected of being a party in a case of corruption. This power is normally with the Home Secretary of the government. Since, however, this power is very important for a proper investigation in many cases, we wanted to give this to an independent authority, like the Lokpal so that the cases could be investigated with better success. On this also, the Home Minister stated that the government was considering this matter and, therefore, this issue may also be discussed at a later stage. The Home Minister also expressed the acceptance of the government of the principle that any loss caused to the exchequer by any corruption should be made good by the corrupt person and the public servant and the private persons involved with him whose property to the extent of the loss could also be confiscated.

In our draft, the Lokpal had the power to transfer, suspend

or remove public servants for infractions that did not merit a full criminal prosecution. The Home Minister, however, stated that transfers, suspension, promotion were within the administrative domain of the government and should remain as such. The real reason for keeping this power with the government is that the executive can then use this power to make officers carry out illegal orders. In my opinion, it should be the function of the ministers to lay down the policy goals and then let the independent bureaucracy implement this policy without having the Sword of Damocles of transfer and suspension hanging on their heads.

Our draft also imbued the Lokpal to make a recommendation in regard to removal of a minister if the facts of corruption required such action. In this connection, Justice Santosh Hegde pointed out that in many cases in spite of facts being known, action for the removal of a minister was not taken.

In the next meeting, Anna Hazare stated that even though one and half months had passed since the deliberations in the Drafting Committee started, only about 25 per cent of the issues had been agreed upon and he felt that valuable time was being lost. He further conveyed his perception that all major issues were being deferred and that only a month remained to finalize the Draft Lokpal Bill. He strongly felt that substantive issues had not been taken up for discussions. He also indicated that major issues like merger of CBI and CVC with Lokpal, bringing the Prime Minister under its purview and inclusion of High Court and Supreme Court Judges also within its jurisdiction were very vital and should be discussed first. He also reminded the Committee that the Bill was required to be finalized within the deadline laid down by the government resolution.

The Chairperson emphasized that the government was committed to introduce the Lokpal Bill in the ensuing Monsoon

Session of the Parliament and there were efforts being made to meet the deadline of 30 June 2011 for the finalization of the Draft Legislation of Lokpal.

If the judiciary was brought within the purview of the Lokpal, the Chairperson pointed out, it may not be possible for it to function independently and such issues had to be analysed more deeply. I, however, straightaway referred to the applicability of the constitutional provisions of Article 226. If any action of the Lokpal was improper, the High Courts and the Supreme Court can always interfere with the same and, therefore, there should be no such apprehension that the powers of the Lokpal could come in the way of independent functioning of the courts.

It became clear that the government was not prepared to pass a strong Lokpal Bill as was being suggested by us, and the Chairperson put forward the excuse that since the government would have to galvanize other parties in the Parliament for passing the Bill, those political parties were also required to be taken on board and their views were also required to be taken into consideration so as to formulate a legislation acceptable to all quarters. This indicated that in spite of the overwhelming desire of the people of the country in favour of the Lokpal Bill as drafted by Anna's team, the government was relying on the politicians to scuttle the spirit of the Bill.

In the deliberation, the Chairperson also expressed his view that the Lokpal would be overburdened if all functionaries from the lowest level to the highest were to be probed and instead should cover only the senior functionaries (joint secretary and above and the ministers).

The problem is that if only high officials and the minister alone were investigated, then they could always escape by stating that the proposal had come from a junior officer and they did not find anything wrong with it on the face of it and, therefore, they just approved in the normal course without looking very deeply into the matter. This would render the Lokpal helpless. On the other hand, if the Lokpal also had the power to investigate the lower officer (who had initiated the proposal) then he/she could be charged with corruption with also a possibility of this lower officer spilling the beans against the higher officials.

On 30 May 2011, HRD Minister Kapil Sibal suggested that contentious issues should be deferred for discussion at a later stage, and in view of paucity of time, there should be an effort to crystalize areas of agreement. For us it was difficult to appreciate that without dealing with crucial issues, how a satisfactory Lokpal Bill could be drafted at all.

In regard to the Bill also providing for Lok Ayuktas in the states, Chairperson Pranab Mukherjee stated that the State Governments had to be consulted for their assent. I, however, pointed out that since the Lokpal legislation was to be in respect of matters in the Concurrent List where the Union Government could legislate and such law would override the State legislations on the same subject once the President gave his assent to such legislation and, hence, there was no reason to consult the State Governments.

Thereafter, there was discussion in regard to the conduct of parliamentarians inside the Parliament and we insisted that the corruption inside the Houses must also be covered by the Lokpal. It may be remembered that at the time when the India-US nuclear deal was being discussed in the Lok Sabha, there were serious allegations of huge monies being paid to various members of Parliament to make them vote in favour of the government and there had been the ugly spectacle of some MPs bringing wads of notes of money on the table of the Speaker in the Lok Sabha. And since the politicians were themselves clearly involved in shady deals, there was hardly any chance of a proper investigation unless there was an institution like an independent Lokpal.

Home Minister P. Chidambaram opposed the shifting of the CBI under the umbrella of Lokpal since it would deny the executive of its own investigative wing and the Jan Lokpal Bill would be upsetting the constitutional framework. I rebutted this by saying that even though investigation was an executive function of the government, it was not the mandate of the Constitution that even matters of corruption be investigated by the government of the day only!

On the issue of covering the prime minister under the Lokpal, Prashant explained out that since the Constitution provided immunity only to the president and governors but not to the prime minister, there was no justification to exclude the prime minister from the ambit of the Lokpal. He also explained that the reason given in Veeraswami's judgement was that since the courts had to exercise powers of judicial review over the actions of the executive, the latter could pressurize the judiciary by launching witch-hunts but since the Lokpal was independent of the executive, the objection of the Supreme Court would also disappear and, therefore, the problem of Veeraswami's judgement would also get solved.

In the next meeting, the representatives of the civil society were absent and only the five Cabinet ministers were present. The Chairperson mentioned that I, Co-Chairperson of the Joint Drafting Committee, had sent a letter indicating their inability to attend the meeting because they were protesting the illegal raid on Ramdev and his supporters, the night before at the Ramlila Maidan.

The last meeting of the Drafting Committee was held on 21 June 2011. On this day the Chairperson requested the Secretariat of the Committee to circulate the Draft Bill on the Lokpal prepared by the government to the members of the Committee. He also invited the representatives of the civil society to circulate the Draft prepared by them.

In regard to the government's Draft Bill, Justice Hegde raised a very important point. He pointed out that even at the stage of preliminary enquiry, even before a First Information Report was recorded, after which the formal investigation starts, this preliminary enquiry was required to be discreet and no opportunity as per criminal jurisprudence was required to be provided to an accused at that stage. HRD Minister Kapil Sibal, however, stated that the proposal was to ensure protection to the public servants especially since the protection afforded under Section 19 of the Prevention of Corruption Act was proposed to be withdrawn. The problem with this is that there is a serious danger in giving an opportunity to an accused person even at a premature stage because in that case, it may hamper proper investigation.

Justice Hegde explained referring to the Supreme Court's decision in the cases of Prakash Singh Badal and Lalu Prasad Yadav that the sanction under Section 9 of the Prevention of Corruption Act was only required to see whether the alleged act under it was committed in the discharge of official duties and, therefore, giving an opportunity to the accused person at a premature stage had nothing to do with the withdrawal of Section 19. However, I pointed out that in criminal law, the only opportunity available to an accused person was before a court of law where the matter reached after charge sheet was filed by the investigative machinery. But, the protection to a government servant against a parallel executive was insisted upon by the Minister of Human Resources Development. This is how the deliberations before the Joint Drafting Committee ended and

Arvind Kejriwal requested for audio tapes being provided to the members of the civil society and the Chairperson stated that the matter would be looked into.

The purpose of Anna's fast to get a Joint Drafting Committee constituted had really failed. Public sentiment was so high initially with the expectations being that the government would find it difficult to resist the proposal of the members of the civil society and would willy-nilly agree to our draft. The government, however, was able to while away the time in fruitless discussions with the thought that public memory is short and so they could ride the storm.

◆

August Phase of Anna Andolan

Rahul Gandhi loses a great opportunity to become the prime minister

After the efforts in the Joint Drafting Committee finally ended in a fiasco, it was time to launch the second phase of the Anna Andolan.

Anna had written to the Prime Minister that if the Parliament did not pass a strong Lokpal Bill by 15 August, he would have no option except to resume his anshan immediately after that day.

As Team Anna believed in the rule of law, it applied for the relevant authority's permission to sit on a hunger strike at JP Park, which is situated in central Delhi. However, the Delhi Police, which is the administrative authority to grant permission, wanted Team Anna to give an undertaking in respect of many conditions. The police wanted the strike to not last for more than three days and the number of participants to not exceed more than 5,000. It was clear that the police was taking orders in this case directly from the Home Ministry, which was headed by P. Chidambaram.

Anna, therefore, sent a letter to the Prime Minister on 13 August asking him to direct the police to grant the permission for the protest fast without any conditions and stating further that he was looking for help from the Prime Minister to get an appropriate place for his anshan for the noble cause of eliminating corruption.

The Prime Minister's office, however, sent a reply the same night stating that his office could not get involved in such a decision-making process and that Anna should address his grievances only to the authorities concerned.

At this stage, it seemed that the Congress government was very confident of defeating the Anna Andolan since they had also, a couple of months earlier, totally vanquished Baba Ramdev's agitation. It seemed the government could not distinguish between Baba Ramdev and Anna, the latter being a true Gandhian, whose team comprised honest and well-intentioned activists.

This led to another political blunder on the part of the Congress leadership, which decided to destroy the moral force behind Anna. So, they authorized Manish Tewari, a senior spokesperson of the Congress, to make a statement:

> *Kishan Baburao Hazare urf Anna, hum tum se puchna chahte hain, tum kis muh se bhrashtachar ke khilaf upvas par baithe ho? Tum khud uper se neeche thak bhrashtachar se lipt ho, aur yeh hum nahin kah rahe hain, Supreme Court ki banai ek jhanch committee ne kaha hai.*

In short, he said that Anna Hazare was no one to lead an anti-corruption movement because Anna himself was drenched in corruption from top to bottom!

The basis of this statement by Manish Tewari was that Anna's

Hind Swaraj Trust had, as a temporary measure, drawn ₹2.2 lakh from its funds on Anna's birthday celebrations—an amount which had been restored to the Trust later. Technically, this was an impropriety because even for a short period, the funds of a Trust cannot be used for a purpose other than that authorized by the Deed of Trust. This technical breach had been pointed out by Justice P.V. Sawant's Commission in which the Trustees had been criticized for this action. The Trustees included Anna, four other National Congress Party ministers and four or five other persons. The Hind Swaraj Trust was formed in 1995 to work for rural development and moral education. Later on, D.M. Sukthankar Task Force dealt with the observations in the Commission's report and he stated that what had happened was only on account of some inadvertence and did not, therefore, call for any action against a person like Hazare, who had been working in the spirit of a missionary to curb corruption by public servants, including ministers. As only a few months before, in April of the same year, during the first phase of Anna Andolan at Jantar Mantar the entire country had seen him on TV for several days and developed great reverence for him. And so the people in the country were outraged at Manish Tewari's statement which, instead of damaging the image of Anna, exposed Congress' arrogance and corruption.

On Independence Day that year, the Prime Minister, in his speech at the Red Fort, referred to Anna's demand that the government accept Team Anna's Jan Lokpal Bill and reminded the latter that the power to make laws had been vested by the Constitution only to the Parliament.

On the evening of 15 August, Anna decided that whether he was granted permission or not, he would sit on a fast at JP Park on 16 August. He decided to go to Raj Ghat to take the blessings of Mahatma Gandhi before starting his fast the next day. As the news of his visit to Raj Ghat in the evening spread, the media reached there as did several thousand supporters of Anna. His image at Gandhi Samadhi, with his eyes closed, was flashed across news channels of the country, and people all over the country expectantly waited for Anna to start his anshan.

Article 19 of the Constitution clearly gives a legal right to all the people in the country to assemble peacefully without arms, and exercise their right to free speech. No order under Section 144 can come in the way of exercise of this constitutional right. In fact, by the Constitution's 44th Amendment, enacted by the Janata Party government in 1978, it has been clearly provided that this right cannot be suspended even during a period of Emergency. The police, therefore, had no right to ask Anna not to sit on a fast in the JP Park as a matter of protest against corruption and for people of Delhi to assemble there. They could not ask Anna to take a written permission on the basis of their administrative order and to comply with the conditions imposed by the police.

As the four days in April earlier that year had shown, Anna Andolan was not only totally non-violent but also disciplined and peaceful. It was the ideal way in which protests should be organized in a country governed by the rule of law. However, it seemed that the government was out to commit one blunder after another.

I own a flat in Supreme Court Enclave in east Delhi which was vacant at the time. So, we had prepared that flat for Anna's stay after he had arrived in Delhi for the fast. Arvind had decided to stay with Anna in the flat on the night of 15 August. Early morning the following day, on the orders of the Home Minister, the police reached the flat and arrested Anna in order to prevent him from going to JP Park to sit on a fast without the permission of the police. As Arvind was with him at the time, he was also arrested; but the two were taken to different destinations. As the news was immediately telecast on TV, all hell broke loose. When Anna asked on what charge he had been arrested, the police officer informed him that he had instructions from the higher-ups to prevent him from going to JP Park.

Team Anna's plan was that before going to JP Park, Anna would once again first visit Raj Ghat to take the blessings of Mahatma Gandhi and then sit on the fast. The police had made extensive arrangements at Raj Ghat to arrest any people assembled there. As soon as I reached Raj Ghat, a police officer accosted me and said that he had to arrest me. He did arrest me, but before asking me to sit in the police bus, he told me that he wanted to be photographed with me and so, we posed for a picture. Let me make it clear that even the members of the police force were sympathetic towards the Anna Andolan as they felt that a true Gandhian was fighting for a great cause and that Team Anna comprised good people who were helping Anna in that cause.

Reports were coming in by then that thousands of people in Delhi were being arrested and sent to different stadiums, where they were treating their detention as a picnic and were singing national songs. As Arvind Kejriwal and Manish Sisodia had also been arrested, they quietly sent word to Prashant not to get arrested in order to lead the movement. So, Prashant arranged a meeting of the Core Committee members of Team Anna at Gandhi Peace Foundation where it was decided that not only a press conference would be addressed, but the action of the government would also be challenged in a court of law.

The Parliament was in session and at 11.00 a.m., the Opposition asked for the suspension of the question hour and launched an assault on the government's action of detaining Anna. The Opposition's main point was that how the government could stop a peaceful non-violent protest and that this constitutionally conferred right could not be taken away by the government in this manner. The entire Opposition had united against the government on this issue. It was this stupidity of the Congress government that created an opportunity for the entire Opposition to unite against it. By evening, the government saw sense and realized the grievous error they had made by arresting Anna and several members of his team along with thousands of other people of Delhi and, therefore, decided to release all of them. Late in the evening, a police officer told me at the Police Officers' Mess that my detention was being ended and I could go home. There is a difference between detention and arrest. So, I had not been formally arrested but had only been detained. On the other hand, Anna, Arvind, and Manish, along with Anna's close associates had been formally arrested sometime in the afternoon and had been taken to Tihar Prison. So, after the decision was taken to release all of them, Anna was informed of the same in the prison. But he wished to not leave the jail until permission was granted to him by the administration for him to sit on a hunger stike at a venue of his choice. With his refusal to leave Tihar, he created a huge problem for the government. He could obviously not be forcibly evicted from Tihar, and that enabled Anna to compel the government to start negotiations.

Anna spent the night of 16 August 2011 on the premises of the Tihar Prison where a huge crowd was collected outside its gate. Sometime in the early afternoon while negotiations were going on and the authorities were finding it difficult to manage the crowd outside the jail, Anna had asked the authorities to allow other members of Team Anna to come and discuss with him the stalemate. So, Prashant, Kiran Bedi, Medha Patkar, Swami Agnivesh, Akhil Gogoi, and Manish Sisodia, as well as Sri Sri Ravi Shankar went to talk to Anna.

As no solution was found, the Core Committee members returned and Prashant announced that Anna would continue his anshan from inside the jail and people were asked to assemble at India Gate in the afternoon to continue their protest. Within an hour, a large number of people had assembled at India Gate to demonstrate that in a democratic republic, it is not only the politicians who count but the people at large also have a voice. Two days after Anna's arrest, a breakthrough came. On 18 August, the Delhi Police granted permission for anshan at Ramlila Maidan for fifteen days without any conditions with it. However, the Maidan first had to be readied for the purpose which unfortunately took time in spite of the municipal corporation staff working at breakneck speed. Anna, therefore, decided to spend another night at Tihar.

On 19 August, Anna left Tihar Prison and went first to Raj Ghat and thereafter reached Ramlila Maidan. In spite of the fact that it was very hot and humid and was also raining intermittently, there was a huge crowd throughout the route to the Maidan. The crowd came from all strata of society—the well-to-do, the middle class, and the poor—with the expectation that something was going to happen which would eliminate corruption from the country. It was a unique movement, the like of which had not been witnessed since the freedom struggle. People took pride in wearing the Anna cap and waving the National Flag, and felt that they were contributing in the shaping of a new India. There were some who even called it a second freedom movement, namely 'freedom from corruption'.

Different sections of society had become impressed with the idea of Jan Lokpal Bill. Film producers, directors, actors, doctors, professors, students, and every class of people were joining the Anna Movement on their own. Musicians and poets were coming forward to create songs to be sung at Ramlila Maidan to create fervour for the Lokpal Bill. While Ramlila Maidan hosted close to one lakh people every day, related events were taking place in many other cities of the country as well because Anna Andolan and the Lokpal Bill had caught the people's attention. The huge crowd was infusing Anna with new energy and he kept addressing the crowd from time to time.

By 23 August, Anna had already fasted for more than a week and the people were beginning to seriously get concerned about his health. It was then that the Prime Minister decided to have serious consultations with Pranab Mukherjee, who was the ablest and most experienced minister in the Cabinet at the time. Thus far, the Anna Andolan was being handled by Chidambaram and Kapil Sibal—whose approach had been totally negative. They had believed that they could destroy Anna and his andolan just as they had done with Baba Ramdev's andolan. They were gravely mistaken, perhaps due to their political inexperience. Therefore, Prime Minister Manmohan Singh met Pranab Mukherjee, P. Chidambaram, and A.K. Anthony, and in the evening wrote to Anna that his objectives were laudable, namely to eliminate corruption, even though their methodology might differ, he expressed his willingness to talk to any person keeping in mind the Parliament's supremacy.

By this letter, a platform was created for discussions and negotiations. After the receipt of this letter, Prashant, Arvind, and Kiran Bedi went to discuss the matter with Pranab Mukherjee. The meeting was reported to be good and Team Anna was hopeful of a breakthrough. Later in the evening, Pranab Mukherjee also appealed to Anna to break his fast stating that his life was precious and that an all-party meeting would discuss the matter next day. He expressed the hope that a mutually acceptable solution could be found. At midnight, a meeting of the Cabinet Committee on Political Affairs was held at the Prime Minister's residence. After this, a meeting of the Core Committee of the Congress was also held.

Meanwhile, Dr N.S. Trehan, who had been looking after Anna during the Andolan, asserted that the lack of food was causing complications in Anna's body and it was necessary for him to be taken to a hospital or an intravenous drip be administered at the Ramlila Maidan itself. Anna, however, at night told the people that his conscience was not permitting him to take an IV, etc. because he had been telling people that he only wanted to live and die for the society. And taking a drip would mean that he was afraid of death, contradicting what he stood for. He also expressed the apprehension that he could be forcibly taken to a hospital to be administered with medicines and a drip; so, he asked his supporters at the grounds to stand at the gate and not permit anybody to enter the Ramlila Maidan but later on retracted this request fearing a clash with the government.

At this point, both the government and Team Anna were worried that if something happened to Anna the people of the country would neither forgive Team Anna nor the government. Both sides wanted an honourable course of action.

Perhaps at the instance of Pranab Mukherjee, Vilas Rao Deshmukh (former CM of Maharashtra), who had known Anna from long before, got in touch with the latter through a phone call and expressed his desire to meet him. Anna agreed to the meeting. So, on 25 August, Deshmukh met Anna and told him that the Prime Minister had saluted him by holding the Parliamentary Committee meeting and had appealed to him to break his fast. What more could he want? Anna felt happy to hear this and told Deshmukh that if the government accepted three of his demands, namely, that corruption in the lower bureaucracy should also be in the Jan Lokpal, a Citizen Charter should be included for time-bound delivery of people's grievances, and should also include Lok Ayukta in the States, he would break his fast.

This was indeed Anna climbing down, but he realized that nothing more was possible at this stage. Team Anna also felt that if these three conditions were accepted by the government then it would mean an honourable way out of the tense situation.

On 26 August, Rahul Gandhi spoke in the Parliament in which he did not appreciate the Jan Lokpal Bill but gave a suggestion that Lokpal should be made a constitutional body accountable to the Parliament like the Election Commission.

On 27 August, Pranab Mukherjee said in the Lok Sabha that Anna's fast had entered the 12th day and the situation was getting out of hands. He insisted that the three issues which had been raised by Anna were genuine and important and, therefore, the Parliament had to consider Anna's three key demands within the constitutional framework. The leader of Opposition, Sushma Swaraj, told Lok Sabha that on behalf of the BJP, she was agreeing to all the three issues raised by Anna. A resolution was then drafted by the government and Kapil Sibal's objection on the wording of the resolution was overruled by the Prime Minister. The debate in the House was stopped and a few lines were read in the form of a resolution and it was unanimously passed by the thumping of the desk.

The message was communicated to Anna by Vilas Rao Deshmukh. He reached Ramlila Maidan and went straight to Anna's small room; after sitting down on Anna's cot, he handed over the Prime Minister's letter. Anna called Arvind, Prashant, and Kiran Bedi, and told them that the Prime Minister's letter had come and he had decided to break his fast the next day at 10.00 in the morning. The announcement was immediately communicated to the people and as Anna went on the stage, all news channels went live on air and the Anna Andolan ended as he broke his fast the next morning.

This is how the second phase ended, not exactly as Team Anna had wanted, but resulting in a significant victory of people's power—humbling a powerful government. The Anna Andolan was the real cause for the Congress' downfall in the next parliamentary election when it lost in a big way.

It occurs to me that if Rahul Gandhi, who has never been in the government and had only been an MP and, therefore, could not have been booked for any corruption charges, had come to Ramlila Maidan, climbed up the stage and addressed the crowd there by telling them that he was with Anna and would help get Anna's Jan Lokpal Bill enacted in the Parliament in order to remove corruption from the government, he would have then and there been acclaimed a great hero. The entire credit of the Anna Andolan would have turned towards him and the Congress would have won with a great majority in the next parliamentary election. Rahul Gandhi could have even emerged as the Prime Minister of India. But whether he would have thereafter succeeded as Prime Minister is another question.

What prevented the Congress from accepting the Jan Lokpal Bill and taking credit therefore? It is well-known that there had been massive corruption in the Congress and all ministers were responsible. They were, therefore, afraid that if the Lokpal of the kind envisaged in the Jan Lokpal Bill drafted by Team Anna was enacted, none of those corrupt ministers would be safe—as an independent Lokpal, free from government's authority of any kind, would surely investigate the matters thoroughly and book them. The corrupt ministers were rightly afraid as nothing could stop them from going to jail if the Jan Lokpal Bill was enacted by them. But, Rahul Gandhi not being in any such danger himself could have taken the initiative to take the credit for the Jan Lokpal Bill and ensured the Congress Party's success in the next election. This could well have been a positive turning point for the Congress. The benefit of the Anna Andolan, since it was able to expose corruption of the Congress ministers in a big way throughout the country, was reaped by the main Opposition party, the BJP, in the next election. The BJP played its cards well without any commitment to enact a bill like the Jan Lokpal Bill if they came to power. And that is the reason that even though some kind of a Lokpal Bill was enacted during the Congress rule, the BJP has not appointed a Lokpal even today.

6
FORMATION OF AAP

After the Anna Andolan's second phase came to an end by August 2011, we took stock of the situation. It was clear that even though under the pressure of the Andolan, the Congress Party had been compelled to bring a Lokpal Bill— it had not met our expectations. Furthermore, to rub salt into our wounds, the Congress leaders would mock us by saying that if the Andolan leaders were keen that their version of Lokpal Bill be passed, they must contest elections, get a majority in the Parliament and then enact a Bill of their choice. In response, we accepted the challenge. We held a meeting at my house in Noida and decided to take the electoral plunge. I am certain the Congress would have regretted this taunt when we brought their tally to a naught in the 2015 Delhi elections.

On 2 October 2012, when the formation of Aam Aadmi Party was announced the meeting was attended by the founding members from all over the country in a massive show of strength. The volunteers went around to collect funds for the launch of the political party and were able to collect a few lakhs or a little more. I had announced in that meeting that I would contribute ₹1 crore. This announcement was received by the assembled members very enthusiastically and laid a proper foundation for starting the work of the party in right earnest.

I also helped in the drafting of the Party Constitution and the vision document. The Constitution of the Party was made different from that of the other political parties by not having a president either at the Central level or at the State or any other lower level, but to have all powers vested in the duly elected committees at different levels which could elect its own convenor to call the meetings of the Committee. This was in order to avoid the emergence of the high command culture (like in the Congress) or centralization of power (like in the BJP).

In November 2012, the founding members met to formally adopt the Party Constitution and elected the National Executive. Meanwhile, a large number of members had been enrolled throughout the country by a very simple method of giving a missed call on a designated number and remitting ₹10 which was the subscription for a period of three years. The Party Constitution contemplated that in due course, starting from the level of the lowest village committee, proper elections would be held and elected committees would replace the ad hoc ones. In the November meeting of the founding members, which were a few hundred, a National Executive was elected and it appointed Arvind Kejriwal as the Convenor.

The next parliamentary elections were to take place in 2014, but the elections to the Delhi Assembly were scheduled to take place in November 2013. The registration of the AAP by the Election Commission was in January 2013 after which the Commission asked the party to select an election symbol from a list of eighty-five free symbols. For selecting a party symbol, another meeting was held at my residence and it was decided that its first preference would be a broom (jhaadu). It was felt that a broom not only symbolized dignity of labour but it could also send a message that the party intended to sweep off the filth which has permeated the government and the legislature.

It was also decided that the launch of the symbol would be formally done in a well-advertised manner in a Dalit colony where the party members would sweep the colony with brooms. I also participated in that function and all of us swept the streets of the Dalit colony. A slogan was also adopted for the forthcoming elections '*Lagegi jhaadu, udhegi dhool, na rahega panja, na rahega phool*', which translates into 'when the broom sweeps, dust will rise and neither the palm nor the flower will survive'. The reference was to the Congress' symbol of a palm and the BJP's of a lotus flower.

While at that Dalit colony, we gave this slogan a musical version and sang it to the accompaniment of a guitar played by a party worker. I was able to contribute to the music because in my childhood days, I had learnt classical music from an eminent Maharashtrian musician in Allahabad.

Before the elections, the candidates were selected by the Executive Committee and then vetted by the Party's Lokpal Panel comprising some independent and highly regarded people. It was only after their clearance that the candidates were given Party tickets for all the seventy seats in the Delhi Assembly.

For collection of funds by means of donations, a website was launched on which every donation, small or big, would be entered date-wise immediately on its receipt, with the name, address, and identity of the donor disclosed. This served a great purpose of creating confidence among the people that the Party would be totally transparent as to from whom it was getting donations and how it was spending them. Even the expenditure was being put on the website. The most significant leaders of the AAP at that time were Arvind, Prashant, and Yogendra Yadav, each of whom enjoyed a very good image and created confidence among the electorate of Delhi. The 2013 election to the Delhi Assembly was a unique one in which members of affluent families not only donated but came forward to work as volunteers as in charge of booths. In fact in many booths, those in charge of both the Congress and the BJP told our people that although they were managing booths for their respective parties, they were also going to vote for the AAP.

A new hope had been generated among the people and when the counting took place, the newly formed AAP had won as many as 28 assembly seats out of 70, reducing the Congress to just eight seats. Even the sitting Chief Minister, Sheila Dixit was roundly defeated by Arvind Kejriwal in her constituency of New Delhi by some 22,000 votes.

When the results came out, all of us were elated and I told the leadership that we must now prepare for the Lok Sabha elections which were going to take place the following year—2014, and that I had decided to donate another sum of ₹1 crore for those elections.

As the Congress was keen to keep the BJP out of power in Delhi, it offered unconditional support to the AAP in the formation of a government in Delhi. Thus, the government got support of 36 members which was a clear majority in a House of 70. The new government then took oath in an impressive ceremony at Ramlila Maidan itself where the Governor administered the oath of office to the Chief Minister and his six Cabinet ministers. At that time, idealism in the party was high and it had proclaimed that the elected members would not take any residence and would take even a reduced pay as MLAs and would also not accept government cars. They would live in a very simple manner like the common man and their stress would be only on serving the people of Delhi.

When the parliamentary elections were announced in 2014, the Executive Committee met again—in which I was called as a special invitee. I felt that time was ripe in which this message of a clean party could go across the whole country and its leaders could campaign all over the country. It was my intention that the question of Arvind Kejriwal resigning as the chief minister of Delhi for contesting an election of the Lok Sabha did not arise because even Narendra Modi as the chief minister of Gujarat at that time had decided to contest the election from Varanasi without resigning from the chief ministership and was continuing to campaign throughout the country. However, I was disturbed when without even consulting me Arvind Kejriwal announced his resignation from chief ministership. He probably felt that he was dependent on the support of the eight Congress MLAs and if a fresh election could take place at that stage itself even in Delhi along with the parliamentary polls, the party was sure to get a clear majority on its own.

Arvind took the bold decision to contest against Narendra Modi from Varanasi but made two colossal mistakes. First, he resigned from the CM position in Delhi (that too without consulting the party members) and second was to stick to Varanasi alone rather than going to other States also to campaign for at least a couple of days in each State. If he had done that, it is my firm opinion, that we would have won at least about 50 parliamentary seats in the country out of 543 and we would have become no.3 party after the BJP and the Congress because no regional party in any State was in a position to get more than 30 or 40 seats. However, the impulsive decisions of Arvind cost us big time. Later, he came to my house and apologized for his mistake of resigning.

In the parliamentary election of 2014, the Modi wave did wonders and the BJP won 282 seats and the Congress won 44. The BJP won all 7 seats in Delhi. Curiously, the only State in which the AAP did well in the parliamentary elections was

Punjab where, out of 13 parliamentary seats, 4 of its candidates won and thus at least the party got represented in the Lok Sabha. None of us had expected that we would do well in Punjab. It seems that the Akali Dal had become quite unpopular on account of many misdeeds of its government and since the Congress had also become quite unpopular on account of its massive corruption, the AAP, particularly after its victory in Delhi in the 2013 elections, got the support of the Punjab electorate.

The huge response to the Anna Andolan and even the conversion of that enthusiasm to electoral votes in the 2013 Delhi elections showed that AAP had massive potential going into the 2014 general election, but the mistakes made by Arvind Kejriwal cost us big time.

In the Varanasi election, while Yogendra Yadav, who is a keen student of every election scene, was clear that Arvind Kejriwal was losing by a couple of lakh votes to Narendra Modi, somehow Arvind Kejriwal was convinced that he was winning hands down and he, therefore, decided to visit Varanasi at the time of counting with the intention of celebrating his victory by a huge victory procession after the results were announced. He had to return quite disappointed. Thereafter, Kejriwal also realized that unlike what he had expected, the Delhi elections would not take place very soon to elect a new Assembly.

As the 2014 elections gave way, it started to become clear that the Central Government was not very keen on having elections in Delhi. As the President's rule continued for almost a year, we filed a petition in the Supreme Court to expedite the holding of a fresh election in Delhi. In the meantime, Arvind Kejriwal, by loss of office, was so frustrated that he decided to make a serious attempt by forming a coalition again with the Congress Party—even by offering them ministership. This move was opposed by Prashant, and the efforts of Arvind Kejriwal totally failed in that regard.

The Congress, at that point, was not prepared to bail out the AAP. However, the case in the Supreme Court had some effect on the Central Government and they decided to hold a fresh election in Delhi in January 2015. By this time, Arvind Kejriwal had become so desperate that he gave up all search for clean candidates and instead gave tickets to opportunists and corrupt individuals. However, in spite of all these things, the lure for the AAP, particularly its support from the lower classes, was still continuing, and at the last moment, when the Congress found itself to be on a weak wicket, it decided consciously for defeating the BJP whom it consideres its main rival and to divert all its votes to the AAP so that the BJP could be defeated in Delhi. The result was a big victory for the AAP—winning 67 out of 70 seats.

Prashant and Yogendra Yadav were not happy at the way tickets were being given so they had decided not to actively campaign for the elections. They were, however, persuaded not to spill the beans till the elections were over, a commitment they honoured. But soon after the elections Arvind Kejriwal realized they would only end up being thorns in his side, and decided to Stalinistically purge them from the party along with their confidants Prof. Anand Kumar and Prof. Jha.

Thereafter, Yogendra Yadav, Prashant, I, and some others who had left AAP decided to launch our own movement under the name of 'Swaraj Abhiyan' so that our original dream of creating a totally honest, transparent, and efficient policy-oriented organization, placing an example before the country, could be realized. A function was held in Gurgaon to launch Swaraj Abhiyan and it was attended by a large number of people including former volunteers of AAP.

Swaraj Abhiyan, in my opinion, for the last two years, has been doing excellent work, particularly in formulating policies for the welfare of different sections of people like farmers and students. We launched a positive programme of bringing people of different religions together by formation of *aman sabhas* in every segment in the country. Recently, we also launched its political outfit called 'Swaraj India'. Yogendra Yadav is the president of Swaraj India and Prashant is the president of Swaraj Abhiyan. Swaraj Abhiyan will continue its non-electoral function by formulating policies and launching movements with the help of other similar organizations that are working in different fields and Swaraj India will contest elections to change the system from the inside. I have very high hopes from both these units.

7
BETRAYAL OF PRINCIPLES BY ARVIND KEJRIWAL

Arvind Kejriwal is intelligent and sharp, and most importantly understands the public mind. At the time of Anna Andolan, I had felt that he was a selfless person and devoted to good causes as well as a good campaigner. An IITian by education, he quit his job in the prestigious Indian Revenue Service (IRS) and wanted to devote all his time to serve the people. I had, therefore, felt that he had the makings of a true leader who could be trusted with leading the new political revolution after the Anna Andolan and the formation of the Aam Aadmi Party.

However, I must admit today that I made a grievous mistake in judging the true character of Arvind Kejriwal in the years 2011 to early 2015. It has now become clear that although he has some qualities, he lacks integrity. It is also now clear that neither did he believe in the founding principles of APP nor in the transformational aims it envisaged. In plain English—Arvind Kejriwal betrayed all the core principles of AAP.

Shortly after the 2014 Lok Sabha debacle, a meeting of the National Executive was to be held in Sangrur in Punjab and to which I was also called as a permanent invitee. One of the subjects to be considered by the National Executive in that meeting was as to whether the Party should contest the forthcoming Assembly elections in Haryana in October that year. Arvind was dead set against the Party contesting those elections. Perhaps, his opposition could be due to the fact that Yogendra Yadav belonged to Haryana and he would be contesting; in the case that AAP won there like in Delhi, Yogendra Yadav could become the chief minister of a full-fledged state and put Arvind Kejriwal's leadership in danger. This was, however, only a speculation, but one which could very well be true.

But many of us were strongly in favour of the party contesting elections for the Assembly in Haryana. The matter was, therefore, put to vote and the majority was in favour of contesting the elections. When this happened, Arvind Kejriwal stated that as the Convener he had the right to overrule even a majority in the National Executive and since he was against the party contesting elections in Haryana, the party would not contest the same. I was shocked and I reminded him that when the party Constitution was drafted by me, I had originally provided for a president of the party at the national-level as well as at the State-level. These presidents had been given special powers in certain eventualities. However, when the Draft Party Constitution was discussed in the National Executive, Arvind had strongly opposed the concept of a president with special powers and said that this would make the party have a high command culture, like that in the Congress. Instead of that, only a Convener of the National Executive Committee and similarly Conveners of the State Executive Committees should be provided for. These Conveners would not have any special rights and their function would be only to convene the meetings of the executive, including emergent meetings, where decisions would be taken preferably by a consensus and by majority, if necessary.

The author talking to social activist Anna Hazare during the fourth day of the latter's indefinite fast for 'Jan Lokpal Bill' in New Delhi.

Photo courtesy: *Outlook*

Anna and his delegation at a meeting of the Joint Drafting Committee.

Photo courtesy: *Outlook*

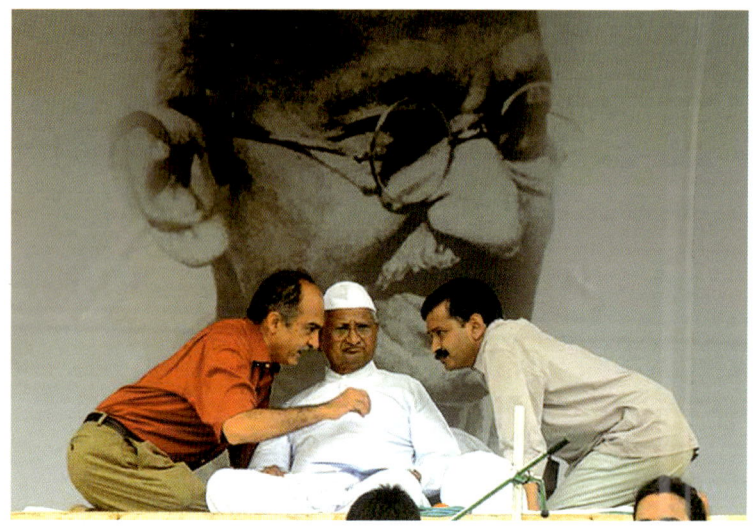

Prashant Bhushan and Arvind Kejriwal accompanying Anna at the Ramlila Maidan.
Photo courtesy: *Outlook*

Anna with his team in 2011 during the Lokpal Andolan.
Photo courtesy: *Outlook*

Members of the joint committee constituted to draft the Lokpal Bill. Left to right in the top row: Union Ministers Pranab Mukherjee (chairman), P. Chidambaram, Kapil Sibal, M. Veerappa Moily, and Salman Khurshid; (left to right in the bottom row) civil society activists Anna Hazare, Shanti Bhushan (co-chairman), Santosh Hegde, Prashant Bhushan, and Arvind Kejriwal.

Photo courtesy: *Outlook*

Civil society members addressing the media after their core committee meeting in Kaushambi, Ghaziabad. Battered by allegations of financial misconduct, the core committee of Team Anna met but ruled out disbanding itself saying it will not be cowed down by government's 'attempts to target its members'.

Photo courtesy: *Outlook*

Civil Society members Kiran Bedi, Shanti Bhushan, Prashant Bhushan, and Arvind Kejriwal during a meeting of the Standing Committee on Lokpal Bill at the Parliament House in New Delhi.

Photo courtesy: *Outlook*

At the book release of Courting Destiny, along with panellists Shri Ram Jethmalani and former Chief Justice of India Shri J.S. Verma.

Wedding of former Chief Justice of India R.S. Pathak in 1955. All of the individuals in the photograph are deceased but the author. From left to right: Chief Justice Satish Chandra, Chief Justice A. Banerji, Advocate Tej Narain Sapru, Advocate Satyendra Nath Verma, Shanti Bhushan, Chief Justice H.N. Seth, and sitting in the groom's chair Chief Justice of India R.S. Pathak.

The author's wife Kumud Bhushan with their daughter Shalini Gupta.

The author's youngest daughter as a toddler at his Allahabad residence.

Childhood picture of Prashant Bhushan and Shalini Gupta, the first two children of the author.

Prashant Bhushan in 1977.

The author's house, 19, Elgin Road, in Allahabad.

The cruise organized on River Yamuna at Allahabad for the author's family and friends for his eightieth birthday celebrations.

The author on the dance stage with world-renowned Kathak dancer Asavari Pawar on the occasion of his youngest daughter Shefali's wedding.

Shefali Bhushan and her husband Jayant Somalkar getting the author's blessings at their wedding on 26 December 2017.

Group photograph of the family assembled to celebrate the author's ninetieth birthday in November 2015.

The author with all his seven grandchildren.

Sector 14, Noida Walkers Club celebrating the author's birthday.

Seen here is the author batting for the Supreme Court Bar Association XI against the Chief Justice of India XI.

The author with his younger son Jayant Bhushan.

The three generations: Shanti Bhushan, Jayant Bhushan, Tushar Bhushan and Amartya Bhushan.

The author with his grandson Sumant Bhushan at the Supreme Court of India.

Group photograph of the Bhushan family assembled to celebrate the author's eightieth birthday in November 2005 at their house in Allahabad.

Shanti's XI—(Shanti Bhushan with his juniors)—his two sons Prashant and Jayant, his two daughters-in-laws Deepa (wife of Prashant) and Reena (wife of Jayant), his grandsons Manav, Sumant, Pavan (sons of Prashant), Tushar and Amartya (sons of Jayant) and Seema (Shanti Bhushan's niece), who studied law at the age of fifty-two.

I reminded Arvind of this and told him that I was surprised that he was then claiming that being the National Convener, he had the right to overrule the majority. On this, his response was that he had never been in any organization where he did not have complete powers to take decisions.

Soon after the Sangrur meeting, I addressed an email to Arvind on 19 July 2014 in which the subject was mentioned as 'Your attempt to destroy the Aam Aadmi Party'. The text of the email is being reproduced in full below:

Till some time back I had a lot of respect for you and always thought that you were inspired with lofty motives and were prepared to make any sacrifice for the country and its people. After watching your recent actions I am getting convinced that you are a totally selfish person only with a selfish personal agenda. You only believe in using and exploiting people only for your self-advancement. I now believe that Aruna Roy rightly believed that you only exploited her for your own ends and did not give her due credit for work in the Right to Information campaign. You have no belief in the concept of swaraj. You have convinced yourself that any achievements in Anna Andolan or in the formation of the Aam Aadmi Party was solely your personal achievements which is nowhere near the truth.

Did you even have the capacity to draft the Jan Lokpal Bill? Could you have even launched the Anna Andolan without Anna or his Gandhian image? You did not have even the rudimentary knowledge of law much less constitutional law to be in a position to make any worthwhile contribution in the joint drafting committee.

It is the sycophants who surround you that keep telling you that all achievements belong only to you and all other people working for the party only have the status of your paid domestic servants. Nobody's opinion counts and you alone have the right to take all decisions for the party.

All committees are only showpieces to defraud the people and throw dust into their eyes to create the illusion that our party is a great democratic party in which decisions are taken collectively. So in reality the party is even worse than Sonia's Congress and would rank with Mayawati's BSP or Mulayam Singh's Samajwadi Party.

While you have contributed both in the Anna Andolan as well as the party like scores of other people whose contribution is in no manner less than yours obviously you do not believe so.

However the monumental mistakes that you have made like holding a dharna as CM and resigning from Chief Ministership without any No Confidence motion being brought have caused such huge damage to the party that it has offset all your earlier contribution and today you have a negative balance in your goodwill account.

A person whose vision is confined to the tiny island of Delhi only has no business to be the All India Convener of a great party like the Aam Aadmi Party. I think if the party has to survive it is essential that you confine yourself to Delhi and resign from the position of All India Convener. A meeting of the National Council be quickly called to elect a new convener.

Unless a quick solution is found I may have to release this letter to the press.

Within two days, on 21 July 2014, I received a response of Arvind Kejriwal which is also, in view of its importance, being reproduced herein below in full. It was in Hindi.

आदरणीय शांतिभूषण जी,

आपका ईमेल मिला। आपने लिखा है कि आपका मुझ पर से पूरी तरह से विश्वास उठ गया है। पहले आप मेरी इज़्ज़त करते थे। अब

आपके मन में मेरे लिए कोई इज़्ज़त नहीं है।

मेरे लिए यह तो मर जाने समान है। मैं आपकी बहुत इज़्ज़त करता हूँ और करता रहूँगा। इसीलिए आपका एक-एक शब्द मेरे लिए महत्त्वपूर्ण है।

मुझमें वे सारी कमियाँ होंगी, जिनका ज़िक्र आपने अपनी ईमेल में किया है। इंसान हूँ। कोशिश कर रहा हूँ कि अपनी कमियों को दूर कर सकूँ। एक ही चीज़ कहना चाहूँगा। मुझमें सौ कमियाँ हो सकती हैं। पर मेरी नीयत साफ़ है। अभी तक जो कुछ भी किया, ईमानदारी और निःस्वार्थभाव से केवल देश के लिए किया। और आगे भी बचा हुआ जीवन देश को समर्पित रहेगा।

आपने मेरा इस्तीफा मांगा है। ये तो बहुत छोटी चीज़ है। जब आप कहगे मैं आधे घंटे में आकर आपके हाथ में सौंप जाऊँगा।

मेरा पूरा प्रयास रहेगा कि मैं ज़िन्दगी में आपका विश्वास दुबारा प्राप्त कर सकूँ।

आपने अपने ईमेल को सार्वजनिक करने की बात कही है। यदि ईमेल सार्वजनिक करने से देश और समाज का ज़रा सा भी भला होता हो, तो आपको उसे तुरंत सार्वजनिक कर देना चाहिए।

आपका,
अरविन्द केजरीवाल

Essentially Arvind replied by saying that he may have a lot of faults (like the one's I alluded him to in my email) but his intentions are good and whatever he does is in the larger interest of the nation.

Immediately on the next day, i.e. on 22 July 2014, I replied to Arvind Kejriwal in which I stated as below:

Dear Arvind,

Your email is looking like a carbon copy of your email to Anna and cannot be taken seriously unless your actions show that you actually continue to believe in the concept of a democratic party. The question whether the party should contest elections in States other than Delhi was referred by the PAC to the National Executive to be decided by taking their views on email. 15 members of the NE were in favour of contesting election in other states also while 2 were against. You refused to accept the decision of the NE. This showed that you also believe what your sycophants do that you alone constitute the party. If you are willing to correct your mistakes you must accept the decision of the NE and declare that you would be willing to show your acceptance by agreeing to go to states for campaigning for at least a day in each state, this alone can show your belief in a democratic party. You must remember that the main objective of the Aam Aadmi Party is to spread the message of clean and ideal politics all over India rather than winning an election and making somebody a Chief Minister. You must also agree to always abide by the majority views hereafter.

In 2012 December while addressing a meeting in Ramlila Maidan I had compared you with Barack Obama and I hope you will not compel me to revise my views.

On hearing from you I shall consider my further steps. I would also advise you to ponder over why important dedicated and able people are deserting the party and even the donations for the party are down to a trickle. Unless we immediately start expanding the party organization and creating roles for scores and scores of able people like Kishore Asthana and others rather than only 4 or 5 of your loyalists the required momentum for the growth of the party cannot be built. Are you willing for this and if so how are you proposing to do this and what are your plans in this connection. Please let me know what are your plans.

Another thing that you must understand is that totally unacceptable means like the recent posters for short term gains are totally against the core principles of our party and must not be repeated in future.

Yours,
Shanti Bhushan

However, Arvind did not send any reply to me thereafter. It was clear that he was not prepared to resign from convenership of the AAP to be replaced by some other person. The person that I had in my mind then as his replacement was Yogendra Yadav who is very competent for the job and was in a position to devote all his time to the party.

When the Delhi elections happened in February 2015, AAP had a landslide victory, capturing a jaw-dropping 67 of 70 Assembly seats; in spite of the unscrupulous practices used by Arvind Kejriwal and his coterie. And the reason for that—the inner conflict regarding the candidate selection, etc.—was not yet revealed to the public.

Having become the chief minister of Delhi again, this time with an overwhelming majority, Arvind Kejriwal decided to get rid of all dissenting voices in the party and did so in the meeting of the Founding Members of the party, which constituted the National Council. This was a surreal, strange meeting in which the regular members were excluded but non-regular members invited. The invitees were barred from carrying their mobile phones inside the venue and burly bouncers were procured in case a physical fracas ensued or maybe just to intimidate the members into compliance and hero-chanting. Arvind, who was present, even provoked the MLAs to launch a physical attack on me in that meeting and got a resolution passed for expelling Prashant and Yogendra along with other important dissenting voices in the party. Arvind destroyed our dreams on that day and converted the AAP from its projection as an ideal political party into his personal fiefdom, which he would rule omnipotent and ruthlessly like Stalin in erstwhile Soviet Union.

We then held a huge convention of party volunteers soon after, in which it was resolved to form a non-political organization 'Swaraj Abhiyan' to work and campaign on political issues with the potential to form a political party in the future, if found necessary.

By this time Arvind had already become an autocrat and did not want his government to be subjected to any scrutiny. Pressure was mounted by the leaders of 'Swaraj Abhiyan' urging Arvind Kejriwal to get a Jan Lokpal Bill passed in the Delhi Assembly, particularly because he had resigned one year earlier on this very issue when he was not permitted to introduce the Bill in the Delhi Assembly as the law required prior approval of the Lt. Governor which he was not prepared to obtain.

Arvind, therefore, decided to bring a bill and have it passed in the Assembly, but a totally different bill, which apart from being quite ineffective to keep a check on his ministers and bureaucrats, was also such that it would not secure the approval of the President in order to become a law. He was keen that there should be no institution which should question any actions of his ministers or bureaucrats. In fact in his version of the Lokpal, the total control in the selection and removal of the Lokpal was tellingly solely in Arvind's hands.

Soon after taking oath Arvind had started misusing all government powers and his ministers were amassing money by corrupt methods under his leadership. He had made appointments on very high salaries of people who had been long associated with him. This was done without any advertisement or selection process. Despite being a knowledgeable person, he knows that the Constitution requires that any appointment to a government post could only be by inviting applications and holding a fair selection. He has been acting completely against the Constitution as applicable to the Union Territory of Delhi and thus making an excellent case for the Central Government to dismiss his government and impose President's rule in Delhi.

I have to hold myself particularly responsible for the dreams of millions of Indians to see an ideal political party lying shattered today because of my mistake in not being able to identify the true colours of Arvind Kejriwal.

8

ATTEMPTS OF HARASSMENT
AFTER THE FAKE CD

When the Joint Drafting Committee for the Jan Lokpal Bill had been constituted on 9 April 2011, its Chairman, Pranab Mukherjee, made a demand that since the government nominees (that is the five ministers) had to declare their assets; the civil society members should also declare theirs. We immediately accepted this demand and all of us sent a list of our assets to the Chairman of the Committee. In my own declaration, I disclosed a large number of immovable properties and also the cash investments in various mutual funds and deposit schemes. As the cash itself amounted to about ₹110 crore, I felt that those who did not know me may perhaps infer that I must have made all this money when I was a Cabinet minister in the Janata Party Government from 1977 to 1979. I, therefore, by way of abundant caution, also enclosed the figures of the income which I had been declaring in my income tax returns for the last ten years, the total of which during that period, viz. from 2000 onwards, came to about ₹150 crore. So, it became clear that these savings were from my legitimate income.

One of the properties, which I had disclosed in my return, was a 12-acre plot in village Kanwari in Tehsil Palampur,

District Kangra, which had been acquired by Kumud Bhushan Education Society in 2010 after obtaining the permission of the government to acquire that land from the villagers, who owned parts of it.

This Education Society was set up by me along with my family members to commemorate my deceased wife, Kumud Bhushan. It was set up in 2004 with the objective to educate the youth on the political and economic issues of the country. This was not going to be an income-generating educational institution, but one of a new kind which was to sensitize the youth of the country on various issues facing the country so that they could keep the concerns of the poor in mind while framing policies on different topics.

On 19 July 2006, the Deputy Commissioner of Kangra had asked the Society to provide the project report as well as the site plan for Essentiality Certificate. The certificate issued by the Director of Higher Education, Himachal Pradesh, on the request of the Secretary of Kumud Bhushan Education Society, recorded that 'the land shall be used only for setting up of an educational institution by the said Society'.

After all the formalities had been fulfilled, the government's permission, as required by law, was granted to the Society to buy land for the establishment of the institution, by a letter dated 2 February 2010 with the condition that the land would be put to such use for which the permission had been granted within a period of two years or such further period not exceeding one year as may be allowed by the State Government, and that the said period would be counted from the date on which the sale deed was registered.

The sale deed of the land purchased by the Society was registered on 4 March 2010. Since the Society had been formed by me and it had purchased the land and got the sale deed registered, I included these 12 acres of land in the return of my assets.

Even though the period of two years from the date of registration of the sale deed was not yet over, several buildings were already constructed which were being used by the Society, and the first workshop for its 'Nuclear Energy Examining the Impacts, Conflicts and Controversies' was held in the main building on 17–19 December 2011.

In spite of the land already being used for the institute of the Society, it applied for an extension of one year on 26 January 2012 to complete the next phase of construction which included the Children's Learning Centre.

It appears that at the behest of some politicians, a notice under sections 118 of the HP Tenancy and Land Reforms Act, 1972 was issued to the Society by the District Collector of Kangra for non-utilization of the land within the stipulated period. The Society promptly replied stating that it had already started using the land for the purposes of the educational institution and the construction of some buildings had already been completed.

On 11 April 2012, the Principal Secretary (Revenue) of the Himachal Pradesh Government, in his letter observed, 'this Department has verified the matter regarding the utilization of the land vide this Department's letter of even number dated 15 March 2012. In view of this, it appears that the applicant Society has already utilised the related land'.

Therefore, it appeared that with this report of the Collector, the entire matter would have rested and no further proceedings were called for. However, after Virbhadra Singh became the Chief Minister of Himachal Pradesh on 25 December 2012, he, for reasons that will emerge later, told the authorities that somehow some action needed to be taken to forfeit the land from the Society as my son Prashant was involved in it. On 22 October

2012, shortly before Virbhadra Singh became Chief Minister, a report appeared in *The Hindu* with the caption 'For Virbhadra Singh, Money Grows on Trees',[4] in which it was mentioned that the former Steel Minister Virbhadra Singh, who was already under scrutiny for the alleged payoffs from the Pramod Mittal-controlled Ispat Industries, was now also under the scanner for some unaccounted cash entries in income tax returns and asset declaration affidavit filed during the nomination process of the Himachal Pradesh Legislative Assembly elections in 2012.

As all the facts mentioned in the report were fully supported by documents, they warranted a criminal investigation. But since the government had not ordered a proper investigation, Prashant wrote to the Vigilance Commissioner and CBI on 11 January 2013 asking them to register an FIR and order a proper investigation into the matter.

This was why Virbhadra Singh, who had since then become the Chief Minister of Himachal Pradesh once again tried to victimize Prashant. Having come to know from my return of assets about the purchase of land in Himachal Pradesh by my Society in 2010, he had given instructions to the various officers under him to somehow get the land forfeited.

It appears that the Collector of Kangra was thereafter summoned to appear before the Chief Minister on 9 December 2013. By this time, Prashant had also filed a Writ Petition in the Delhi High Court in November 2013 praying for a Writ of Mandamus directing the CBI and the Director General Income Tax (Investigation) to initiate an investigation under the supervision of the High Court, into charges of money laundering, corruption, possession of disproportionate assets, criminal misconduct, etc.,

---

[4]Singh, Shalini, 'For Virbhadra Singh, money grows on trees', *The Hindu*, 22 October 2012, https://www.thehindu.com/news/national/for-virbhadra-singh-money-grows-on-trees/article4023305.ece

against Virbhadra Singh. On 17 September 2014, the District Collector of Kangra at Dharamshala passed a detailed order stating that the land purchased by the Society be vested in the Government of Himachal Pradesh, free from all encumbrances, along with structures, if any, on the said land. The operative part of the order is extracted below:

> *Hence the rigours of Section 118 (2) (h) of H.P. Tenancy and Land Reforms Act 1972 is attracted in this case and I order for the vestment of the land purchased by the respondent Society situated at Kohal Kamlehr, Mouza Kandwari, Tehsil Palampur, District Kangra comprising in Khasra Nos. 114, 115, 182 and 183 area measuring 4-68-28 Ha with the Government of Himachal Pradesh free from all encumbrances along with the structures if any there on the said land.*

The Society promptly filed an appeal with the Divisional Commissioner of Kangra, which is still pending before him since then. He keeps on adjourning the case again and again because it seems that he is not willing to be a party to an illegal order and may be waiting for the term of the Chief Minister to be over.

The various officials concerned keep on privately telling Prashant that they are aware that there is nothing in the government's case against the Society but they have to show that they are doing something about it.

This entire episode demonstrates how government powers are misused at the behest of politicians for their own ends and how government officials, who can be victimized by the politicians for not carrying out their diktats, have to make effort to escape from being victimized. It is, however, good to know that most of these officials are well-intentioned and do not want to transgress the law to victimize an innocent person on the illegal orders of politicians, and many times, they have to walk a tight rope.

9

MY APPEARANCES AGAINST CORRUPT CHIEF MINISTERS

Politicians become chief ministers after a long political struggle in lower positions. When they do become chief ministers, they regard themselves as demigods and feel that on account of the immense powers they enjoy, every person should be at their beck and call even if that they are totally corrupt.

In my professional career, I have maintained two principles regarding powerful politicians: First, if I am prima facie convinced that they are corrupt, I refuse to appear for them when approached in spite of the fact that in the past I might have represented them in courts. Second, if a chief minister wants to meet me in connection to a pending case, he has to come to my office and cannot invite me to meet him at his office.

When I was representing the Kerala Government before the Inter-state Water Dispute Tribunal, which had gone on for many years, and I had made my appearance at various places before the Tribunal on behalf of the Government of Kerala, even cross-examining the witnesses produced by the Tamil Nadu Government or the Karnataka Government in which they tried to show their claims for more water sharing, it was my contention on behalf of

102 • *Shanti Bhushan*

the Kerala Government that the dispute had to be decided on the basis of overall benefit to the nation, and if giving some water to one State meant more overall benefit to the nation—that be kept in view. I was contending that if a particular amount of water was given to Kerala, it could be utilized for two purposes: first, for generation of an adequate amount of electricity because of the hills there and the River Kaveri passing through those hills; and secondly, after generating power from that water, the same could also be utilized for irrigating the lands of Kerala to the west of the hills. During the hearing, A.K. Anthony, who was the Chief Minister of Kerala at the time, expressed a desire to the counsel who were assisting me that he would like to meet me in Delhi at the Kerala House where he used to stay. When this request was conveyed to me, I told my briefing counsel for the Kerala Government that it was my principle that when a client wanted to see me, he had to come to my office and not vice versa. This was conveyed to the Chief Minister Anthony. Evidently, he did not like it and gave instructions that the senior counsel should be changed.

◆

When MGR passed away, there was a dispute in regard to political succession after him and the disputants were Janaki Ramachandran, the wife of the deceased Chief Minister, and J. Jayalalithaa, who had for a long time been MGR's co-star in many successful films. The matter in regard to possession of the party office came to the Supreme Court and I was briefed to represent Jayalalithaa in that litigation. My submissions before the Supreme Court on her behalf succeeded and she won the dispute to the party office. She felt so obliged on this success that on my next visit to Chennai (Madras, then), to appear in some other case in the High Court, she invited me for tea at her Poes Garden residence. When I met her one-to-one for the first time and talked to her, I found her to be an extremely intelligent person who could understand the problems immediately and I could see that she would become a successful politician.

Later, when Jayalalithaa was the Chief Minister, a corruption case was filed against her—and when that matter came to the Supreme Court, her counsel in the Supreme Court approached me to represent her. However, by this time, I was convinced on the basis of material that had come in the press related to her corruption that she indeed had become a corrupt chief minister. Since it was my principle not to represent corrupt politicians in any case of corruption, I politely declined her brief. On the other hand, when subsequently I was approached by the Tamil Nadu Government to represent it in the Supreme Court against her in that corruption matter, I accepted the brief and argued the matter. Although I had represented Jayalalithaa in her earlier case regarding the possession of the party office, that had nothing to do with the corruption case later against her as the chief minister and, therefore, there was no technical difficulty in my accepting a brief to appear against her.

Another instance of my refusing to appear was when Janki Ballabh Patnaik, Chief Minister of Odisha (Orissa, then) had personally come to my office in Niti Bagh, New Delhi, to ask me to appear for him in a corruption case against him. I politely declined to represent him.

Even in the case of Lalu Prasad Yadav, before his corruption case in the fodder scam emerged, I had been regularly representing Lalu's Bihar Government in the Supreme Court on the instructions of the government's advocate on record. So, when the matter relating to his corruption came to the Supreme Court, the same advocate on record of Lalu's government approached me to represent Lalu before the Supreme Court in that matter also. Since I had clearly formed the impression that Lalu had become a corrupt chief minister, I again politely declined the invitation. When this news reached George Fernandes who was spearheading the corruption case against Lalu Prasad, he personally came to my residence at Niti Bagh requesting me to accept the brief on his behalf, although he could not afford my fees. I told him that fighting corruption was my mission and I did not accept fees for fighting cases in which I was pitted against corrupt politicians. I, therefore, appeared against Lalu Prasad in the matter on behalf of George Fernandes and prevented Lalu Prasad from getting any relief in the Supreme Court. Obviously, after this, the question of my being briefed for the Bihar Government in any of their cases could not arise and, therefore, I ceased appearing for them thereafter.

In 2013, when Lalu's trial before a Special Judge had almost been completed in spite of various counsel, including Ram Jethmalani, taking adjournments after adjournments and inordinately delaying the trial, an objection was raised that the judge trying the case against Lalu Prasad was related to Nitish Kumar, Lalu's then opponent, and some photographs of the judge attending some functions in Nitish Kumar's family were relied upon in that connection. The judge in question, however, refused to recuse himself on that account, and the matter was brought to the Supreme Court by Lalu Prasad, and several hearings took place before a bench headed by Chief Justice P. Sathasivam. Lalu Prasad was being represented by Ram Jethmalani and it appeared that the judges were inclined to transfer the case to a new Judge and they asked the CBI's counsel and Lalu Prasad's counsel to give the court an agreed list of some district judges from whom the bench might select one to whom the case could be transferred. At this point, the original complainant, Lallan Singh approached me to appear in the matter, and I accordingly appeared before the bench. When the judges referred to their last order and asked for the agreed list of judges, I made a strong intervention and told the bench that there was no case for transfer to another judge at that point in time on the grounds the transfer was being asked for. I further argued that if at this point, the case of a powerful politician like Lalu Prasad got transferred from the judge, who had been trying it for years, it would send a message across the country that a powerful politician could always find ways to escape justice. My strong intervention had the desired effect and the judges changed their minds and passed an order rejecting the plea of Lalu Prasad Yadav.

A news item then appeared in the press with the caption, 'Lalu's trick fails, SC refuses to change trial judge'. The article is being reproduced below in view of the importance of that order:[5]

Lalu's trick fails, SC refuses to change trial judge

With the supreme court dismissing the petition of former Bihar Chief Minister Lalu Prasad Yadav who sought to change the Special CBI judge in Ranchi hearing the fodder scam case, there is a strong possibility of political equations in Bihar undergoing a sea change.

The three-member SC bench headed by Chief Justice P Sathasivam has also directed the special CBI judge at Ranchi to deliver the verdict as soon as possible. The turn of events came quite unexpectedly as Yadav has been desperately resorting to legal stratagems to stall the verdict of the trial court.

Though Yadav did not find sympathetic hearing from the Ranchi High Court where his petition of changing the judge on the ground of 'impartiality' was dismissed, he

---

[5]Singh, Ajay, 'Lalu's trick fails, SC refuses to change trial judge', *Governance Now*, 13 August 2013, https://www.governancenow.com/news/regular-story/lalus-trick-fails-sc-refuses-change-trial-judge

managed to evoke a degree of sympathy from the Supreme Court in two earlier hearings last month. When Chief Justice Sathasivam asked the prosecution and the accused to shortlist the names of the judges in case the court ordered thus, it seemed that the apex court was actually inclined to grant this extraordinary relief for Lalu.

It caused some consternation in the judicial and political circles. It was being seen as yet another success for Lalu in the way he has manipulated the legal process to delay the case. If the court had ordered a retrial when the trial court had set a date for judgment, merely because the judge happened to be a distant relative of a JDU minister who had just lost an election to Lalu's lieutenant, it would have put the whole judicial process behind by at least a decade. And set a rather sad precedent. An intervention application filed by the original petitioner in the fodder scam, Rajiv Ranjan alias Lallan Singh, drew the attention of the SC bench comprising Justice Sathasivam, Justice Ranjana Desai and Justice Ranjan Gogoi towards the dilatory tactics of Lalu.

On August 6, veteran lawyer Shanti Bhushan intervened for Lallan and tore apart the arguments of Yadav that the trial would be unfair if the presiding special judge of the CBI court was not changed. He effectively contradicted the insinuation that the judge would be biased as he was a relative of Yadav's rival and a minister in the Nitish Kumar Government. Raising serious questions about the unintended fallout of any move to change the trial court judge, Shanti Bhushan pointed out that such a move would convince people that politicians in the country can never be hauled up before the courts no matter how serious their crimes.

The SC judgment on Tuesday is a major setback to Lalu who is still reckoned in Bihar as a formidable political force.

Given the fact that the trials in the fodder scam have seen scores of convictions, Lalu's political fate could be hanging on this verdict. If he is convicted in the case, he would not only be jailed but also forbidden to contest the forthcoming Lok Sabha elections. A recent apex court judge has held that the convicted legislators cannot contest elections.

Political parties as one have resolved to either file a review petition or amend the law to overturn the SC's direction on the issue. Given the popular resentment over such a move, it appears quite difficult for the union government embroiled in corruption cases to resort to tactics which will be seen as justifying corruption. In such a scenario, Lalu's conviction in the fodder scam would invariably mark the beginning of an end for one of Bihar's most charismatic and controversial political personalities. And this will set the stage for new political realignments which will have significant bearing on the national scene.

10

SANJAY DUTT WAS INNOCENT

In the summer of 1994, I had appeared for Sanjay Dutt before the Special Judge in the Arthur Road Jail for his bail application. I had been briefed by Sunil Dutt (the legendary film actor and Sanjay Dutt's father) and had gone to Mumbai for the case. The day on which I had to appear in the court, early in the morning I developed an excruciating pain in my back due to a slipped disc. It was impossible for me to move and the pain was unbearable. I rang up the hotel management to send for medical assistance. When the doctor came, I told him that it was crucial for me to appear today to argue for Sanjay Dutt's bail application and that it would be great if the doctor could give me a powerful analgesic to relieve me of the pain for at least for some hours, so that I could argue the matter. The doctor agreed and gave me an injection which completely relieved me of the pain in about forty-five minutes and I was able to go to the court. The orders were reserved by the Special Judge after hearing the arguments. In the evening, Sunil Dutt took me to the Breach Candy Hospital to be admitted for treatment but I told him that I prefer to get treated in Delhi and that I should be given the same powerful analgesic so that I could travel back. They did so and I reached Delhi in the evening that day. The doctors at AIIMS advised me complete bed rest for at least one month. So, thereafter I could not appear for Sanjay Dutt in the Supreme Court for his bail application.

Sanjay's case was full of twists and turns and a brief chronology is as follows:

12 March 1993: Mumbai rocked by 12 bomb blasts between 1.33 p.m. and 3.40 p.m., which killed around 157 people and injured another 713.

19 April 1993: Police escorted Sanjay Dutt on his arrival from Mauritius saying that an AK-56 rifle was found at his residence from the consignment of arms smuggled before the blast. He was arrested.

26 April 1993: Sanjay Dutt admitted to the charges in his confession.

3 May 1993: Sanjay Dutt released on bail.

4 July 1994: Bail cancelled and he was rearrested.

16 October 1995: After spending nearly sixteen months in jail, Sanjay Dutt was again released on bail.

July 2007: Sanjay Dutt convicted for illegal possession of a 9mm pistol and an AK-56 rifle, but acquitted of very serious charges under the Terrorists and Disruptive Activities Act and sentenced to six years' jail term.

2 August 2007: Sanjay Dutt was arrested again and taken to Yervada jail in Pune.

20 August 2007: Sanjay Dutt was granted bail by the Supreme Court.

21 March 2013: The Supreme Court dismissed the appeal of Sanjay Dutt and reduced his sentence from six to five years as that was the minimum sentence prescribed for the offence under the Arms Act for which he had been convicted and he was asked to surrender within four weeks.

When I read the judgement, I found that the main defence that Sanjay Dutt could have availed of (that being his right to private defence) had not been argued by his counsel. I also felt that even on the findings recorded by the Supreme Court, he was clearly innocent and was entitled to acquittal.

I, therefore, wrote an article immediately which was published by *The Hindu* on 26 March 2013 under the caption 'This plot needs a new ending'. I am reproducing the entire article below which is self-explanatory:[6]

> When the law says nothing done in the exercise of the right of private defence is an offence, it would be a travesty of justice to send Sanjay Dutt to jail.
>
> In Paragraph 70 of its judgment in Sanjay Dutt's appeal, the Supreme Court has observed thus: 'In the case of Sanjay Dutt, the Designated Court took a view on the basis of his own confession that the weapons were not acquired for any terrorist activity but they were acquired for self-defence, therefore, acquittal was recorded in respect of charge under Section 5 of TADA. We fully agree with the same.'
>
> **Not punishable**
>
> Section 96 of the Indian Penal Code provides: 'Nothing is an offence which is done in the exercise of the right of private defence.' Section 40 of the IPC provides that Chapter 4 of the code is applicable to not only offences punishable under IPC but also to offences punishable under other special laws like the Arms Act, 1949, Section 96, which has been extracted above, is in Chapter 4 of the IPC. It is thus clear that if the weapons for the possession of which Sanjay Dutt has been convicted under the Arms Act

[6]Bhushan, Shanti, 'This plot needs a new ending', *The Hindu*, 26 March 2013, https://www.thehindu.com/opinion/lead/this-plot-needs-a-new-ending/article4548129.ece

had been acquired for self-defence, their possession without a licence would not, on the findings of the Supreme Court, in itself constitute a punishable offence.

This important aspect of the matter has been completely overlooked by the Supreme Court and constitutes a clear error of law on the face of the judgment itself. A review of the judgment on this ground would clearly lie and should be allowed by the same bench of the Supreme Court to which it will go.

However, generally, the judges of the Supreme Court hesitate to accept that they have made a mistake even when they have made one. It is only really great and eminent judges who do not hesitate in accepting their own mistake because it is human to error.

In any case, even if the Bench rejects the review application, it would be open to Sanjay Dutt to file a curative petition, which right was evolved by the five-judge Constitution Bench of the Supreme Court in Rupa Hurra's case (2002 (4) SCC 388).

This curative petition can be filed only after the remedy of a review petition has been availed of and has been unsuccessful. According to the law laid down by the Supreme Court in Hurra's case, such a petition will not go before the same bench which had decided Sanjay Dutt's case but will go before a larger bench which will have to include not only the Chief Justice of India but also the two senior most judges of the Supreme Court after the Chief Justice. It is this larger bench that will have to decide the curative petition. There is no reason to feel that when this new bench decides this question of law, which is so clear, it will not set aside the conviction and sentence of Sanjay Dutt.

The evidence in the case fully establishes that well before the Bombay blasts (12/03/1993), for which the entire trial had taken place, there had been serious riots in Bombay (December 1992–January 1993). Subsequent to the demolition of the Babri Masjid (06/12/1992), Muslims of Bombay were being targeted by the Shiv Sena and its mobs. The evidence further shows that Sanjay Dutt's father, Sunil Dutt, and the whole family was helping to protect innocent Muslims being targeted by the Shiv Sena mobs. This had also occasioned an attack on Sunil Dutt himself (January 1993) for which he had written to the authorities.

Under real threat

It was evident that there was a clear danger of a mob attack on Sanjay Dutt and his family, including his parents. An attack by such a mob could not have been deterred except by the threat of an automatic weapon and it was for this very reason that Sanjay Dutt had agreed to acquire the automatic weapon, namely, the AK-56 Rifle (in mid-January 1993). It is also clear that no private person is ever granted a licence for acquiring an automatic weapon and therefore the only possible way for Sanjay Dutt to protect his family against a mob attack was to acquire the automatic weapon through alternative channels. So long as the purpose of acquiring this automatic weapon was to defend his family from a mob attack, as both the designated court and the Supreme Court clearly found on the evidence recorded, this act of acquiring the possession of the automatic weapon would not constitute the offence as shown above from the relevant provisions of the IPC.

The relevant facts and circumstances in which Sanjay Dutt had to acquire the automatic weapon have been noticed in paragraph 74 of the judgment which is reproduced herein below:

'It was also contended from the side of the appellant that in the year 1992–93, the appellant and his family members were involved in helping people residing in riot affected areas, more particularly, Behrampada, predominantly having a Muslim population which was objectionable to a certain group of persons who were of the opinion that the Dutt family was sympathisers of only the Muslim community. In fact, this led to an attack on Sunil Dutt in January 1993, as well as threatening phone calls were being received at their residence, including threats to the family members being killed as well as the sisters of the appellant being kidnapped and raped. This led to a great and serious apprehension that an attack could be perpetrated upon the Dutt family in view of the fact that Shri Sunil Dutt had already been attacked. This apprehension was clearly set out in the letter of Shri Sunil Dutt to the then DCP of Zone VII dated 06.01.1993, wherein he asked for enhancing security arrangements further and for more police protection at his house as deposed by PW-219 in this case.'

It was in view of these circumstances that the Supreme Court reduced the sentence given to Sanjay Dutt from six years to five years as five years was the minimum prescribed term under Section 25(1A) for being in possession of an automatic weapon.

Honourable person

It is clear from the above facts that Sanjay Dutt is an honourable person who according to the Supreme Court had made a voluntary confession setting out all the facts and circumstances in which he had acquired the automatic weapon, the confession which the Supreme Court found to be voluntary and true and his conviction is also based on his own voluntary and truthful confession.

It would be a travesty of justice if such a person has to go to jail now merely because an important provision of law has been overlooked by the Supreme Court. Either the Supreme Court in a review or curative petition or any other constitutional authority which is entitled to grant him relief must do justice by making an order so that an honourable person like Sanjay Dutt does not have to suffer any more.

As my article would clearly demonstrate, on the findings recorded by the Special Judge and the Supreme Court that he had acquired and kept the fire arms only for self-defence as his family was under great threat from Shiv Sena mobs. Based on the findings of the Supreme Court, he should have been acquitted. In my opinion, it was clearly an error of his counsel and the Supreme Court should not have convicted him. But, as mentioned in my article, it is only great judges who are prepared to admit their mistakes and correct themselves. Evidently, Justice Sathasivam and Justice Chauhan were not among those great judges.

Many a times, it has happened in the past and, perhaps, it will happen in future also that innocent people are sent to jail. If during the appeal I had been contacted to appear in this case, I would have definitely argued the point of his right to private defence.

11

THE INDIAN NATIONAL CONGRESS:
A PARTY OF, BY, AND FOR THE GANDHIS

Mahatma Gandhi and Jawaharlal Nehru—they were two important leaders responsible for India's freedom and also for the establishment of a democratic way of life in India. But, when we talk of the Nehru–Gandhi dynasty, the reference is not to Mahatma Gandhi's name. He was a Gujarati; and the name in Nehru–Gandhi has nothing to do with him. It comes from Indira Gandhi's husband, Feroze Gandhi, who was a Parsi. He was a Congress worker during the freedom movement and being the husband of Indira Gandhi, lived with Pandit Nehru where the freedom movement headquarters were located. He worked closely with the Nehru family and, therefore, came in contact with Indira Gandhi and they fell in love and got married in 1942. I am not quite sure to what extent Indira Gandhi was attracted to Feroze Gandhi. On account of the name he bore, it is a possibility that she may have married him in order to have 'Gandhi' in her name and so that people were likely to associate her name with Mahatma Gandhi, which would give her some political weightage. It is a possibility which cannot be discounted.

The fact that Indira Gandhi attached a lot of importance to a name in her political fortunes became evident when I was arguing the election case against her in the Supreme Court in 1975. When the case began, the CJI, who was presiding over a five-judge bench, read the names of the parties. Indira had always been known as Indira Gandhi, and never as Indira Nehru Gandhi. So, when the Chief Justice found her name being mentioned as Indira Nehru Gandhi in the election petition which I had filed against her, he put a question to me, 'Mr Shanti Bhushan, why have you named her Indira Nehru Gandhi?' He thought I was mocking her by naming her Indira Nehru Gandhi. I stated, 'My Lord, I named her Indira Nehru Gandhi in the election petition because she contested the election under this name.' Everyone in the court was surprised that Indira Gandhi had mentioned her name in the nomination paper as Indira Nehru Gandhi. But that simply shows that she knew the importance of exploiting that name. She wanted to exploit the name of Gandhi, and not let go of Nehru either. Many in India might not have known then that Feroze Gandhi was a Parsi, and would have easily believed that she was related to Mahatma Gandhi.

The Nehru–Gandhi dynasty was started not by Jawaharlal Nehru, rather it was his father Motilal Nehru. Senior Nehru was a very competent, sharp, and witty lawyer. He was also very prosperous, being the richest lawyer in India. Motilal Nehru was also a liberal, contesting elections to the legislative council of India along with other leaders having liberal views. He did not have socialist views like Jawaharlal Nehru. Normally a son inherits ideas from his father and not the other way round but the case of Motilal Nehru was an inversion of dictum as he got his ideas from his son, Jawaharlal.

Motilal was devoted to his only son, whom he even sent to Cambridge for higher education. Jawaharlal Nehru was an Englishman in many ways—his thinking and ideas. He imbibed his ideas of democracy in England. He also had friends with extreme left views in England, and it was due to them that he developed his ideas of socialism. He assimilated those ideas before he returned to India.

Jawaharlal Nehru's heart was for the common man. He had walked through the hot, dusty villages of Uttar Pradesh in summer on foot to learn what India was all about. He had written *The Discovery of India* because it was through his travels that he came in close touch with the poor population of India. He understood their ways of life, their problems, their aspirations and, therefore, all his mental make-up and attitude in politics was built by that close contact with the common man. He was a true leader. He deserved to be the prime minister and he was in fact a very distinguished one for seventeen years—from 1947 to 1964. He not only played a very important part in the freedom movement through his eloquence, but he could also make a common man understand complex propositions by reducing them to simple things, even through illustrations.

I have seen Motilal Nehru, but not met him. But I have met Jawaharlal Nehru and interacted with him, even if only briefly. It was Indira Gandhi who had introduced me to Jawaharlal Nehru in 1957. My family, of course, was very close to the Nehru family because my parents lived in Allahabad too. My father had even gone to jail with Jawaharlal Nehru during the 1921 movement. My mother was the closest friend of Kamala Nehru, Jawaharlal Nehru's wife. Kamala Nehru generally went around only with my mother. She did not normally get a car for her personal use from the Nehru household because out of both their cars one was appropriated by Motilal Nehru and the other by Jawaharlal Nehru and Vijay Lakshmi Pundit. So, Kamala Nehru went about in our car; we owned an old Ford 8 at the time.

So far as Indira Gandhi was concerned, my elder brother, who was seven to eight years older to me and almost the same age as Indira Gandhi, was much fascinated by her and used to go to Anand Bhawan almost every day as a young boy. Though my family had a lot of interaction with theirs, I in particular did not have much interaction with them except in 1957 when I campaigned for Jawaharlal Nehru with Indira Gandhi in her car. At that time, I had realized that Indira Gandhi was a very intelligent lady. During the campaign, I had put a question to her, 'Why is it that in Kerala, Congress is not winning and it is the Communist Party which is winning there?' Pat came the reply from her, 'Educated unemployment.' She said that there might be unemployment elsewhere [too] but that would not give rise to communism. It is only in a place where educated people are unemployed that communism will prosper and because in Kerala there is lot of education and educated are unemployed, communism has grown there. So, I found that she was very intelligent. She had grown up during the freedom movement, and had imbibed the Congress culture, the political theories, etc., since childhood.

Indira Gandhi was the only daughter of Jawaharlal Nehru. A part of this great family naturally made her a very dominant person. She was intelligent, bold, and also very ruthless. May be in order to succeed in politics you have to have the quality of being ruthless. Her ruthlessness was exemplified when she became prime minister in 1966. She was responsible for defeating her own party's candidate, Neelam Sanjiva Reddy, for the presidentship of India by setting up V.V. Giri and working for his victory—also the reason why the Congress split. During the Emergency, no other political leader but Indira Gandhi could have dared to put in jail a person of the stature of Jayaprakash Narayan or even tall leaders like Morarji Desai and others. She was so tough and ruthless that if she had wanted something, she would go all out for it without thinking of any scruples. No other leader could have freed Bangladesh. It was only her idea, but it was so ruthlessly executed that she was able to liberate Bangladesh. Even one of the greatest leaders of Jan Sangh, Atal Bihari Vajpayee had to proclaim her as 'Durga'.

Indira Gandhi had great qualities, but she also had great faults. That was why an election petition was filed against her, and I cross examined her for two days. The challenge to her was the 1971 election, of which the judgement came in 1975. I had to prove that she was acting against the law by taking the help of people in the government for making her candidates win. So, I caught hold of a document from the Congress headquarters— which, after the split in the Congress, was with our party, the Opposition Congress. Therefore, I sent a word there telling them that Mrs Gandhi had been Congress President from 1957 onwards for several years. So, they should find some documents which will throw doubt on her credibility. They sent me a bunch of documents and I selected a few. One of the documents that I selected was from 1959. In 1959, there had been a by-election in Himachal Pradesh when Mrs Gandhi was the Congress President, and the Lt. Governor there had written a letter to her saying, 'You had entrusted a very difficult task to me, your candidate was very weak, but I have been successful in making your candidate win.' She had initialled that letter in the margin. I put that document to her in cross-examination, first asking her whether those were her initials. She accepted that those were her initials. She accepted to having received the letter and then I asked her to read it aloud. After she read it, I asked her which task it was that she had entrusted to the Lt. Governor of Himachal Pradesh for which he had said that her candidate was very weak, but he had managed to make him succeed. She was very upset and had responded saying it must have been something to maintain law and order. I argued that since she was the only Congress President and not in the government, how was it possible for her to entrust the maintenance of law and order to the Lt. Governor? So, it became quite clear and I ultimately put to her that right from the 1950s, she had been in the habit of taking the help of people in the government to make her candidates win and that was why she used the government people in that particular election also.

Her personality included some good aspects but also some flaws. The flaws were probably on account of the fact that she was a little insecure by nature. In politics, so long as you are in power you are fine, but if you are not in power and if you do not have any other vocation, you feel insecure because politics becomes your profession. It is my belief that politics should not be a full-time profession. Whenever you have to give up a political office, you should switch back to your permanent profession. In 1975, when her election was set aside, she should have promptly resigned rather than try to continue by amending the Constitution and putting people in jail. It was not a wise thing to do; and she paid the price for it. After the Emergency was over and the election was held in 1977, such an election probably has never been held in any part of the democratic world. The whole of North India which accounted for two third seats in the Parliament, and the Congress Party under her leadership when she was the prime minister, failed to secure more than one seat out of the 350. It was a resounding victory of the Opposition Party which had been organized by Jayaprakash Narayan.

After Indira Gandhi, came her son. She did not originally have plans for Rajiv Gandhi to enter politics. Poor Rajiv, he was not even interested in politics and was an airline pilot instead; and he was happy being that. He had also lived in England for a few years, where he had met Sonia Gandhi. He fell in love with her and then got married to her. Rajiv lead a peaceful life as an airline pilot and he was very satisfied with it. The political legacy of Indira Gandhi was to be bequeathed to her younger son, Sanjay Gandhi. He was a ruthless politician, totally unscrupulous, but unfortunately he died in an air crash the same year as Mrs Gandhi came back to power. She had no choice except to force poor Rajiv to start learning the tricks in the trade of politics. He was virtually dragged into politics as a reluctant politician and when Indira Gandhi was assassinated in 1984, he was made the prime minister.

Rajiv Gandhi, as I said, was essentially a decent person. He would have been an honest person; but when he entered politics, his colleagues in the Congress taught him that without corruption you cannot succeed and that is why Bofors happened, which is still the ghost pursuing the Nehru–Gandhi dynasty. From time to time, it continues to raise its head. Rajiv Gandhi, of course, also had to pay the price of his misadventure in Sri Lanka. During the 1991 election campaign in which there were hardly any chances of his coming back to power, it was not likely that the Congress could have secured a clear majority, but as he died during the election campaign, it turned the sympathy factor in favour of the Congress and that is why ultimately it did succeed, although it did not get even a simple majority. Narasimha Rao, being a clever man, succeeded as the prime minister. With all kinds of political tricks, he did complete his period of five years as prime minister.

After Rajiv Gandhi's death, Sonia Gandhi entered the scene. Initially she had been totally reluctant to enter politics. But the Congress people had wanted to make her the prime minister when Rajiv Gandhi died but she had declined. That was in 1991, but later in 1998 she decided to take over as the Congress President and was also willing to become the prime minister. But in 1998, unfortunately, she could not secure a majority. Her chance came in 2004. Having lived with Indira Gandhi for such a long period, she had understood that the common man mattered in democracy, particularly in Indian democracy and that is why even though the BJP and the NDA were sure of succeeding in the 2004 general election on the plank of 'Shining India', Sonia Gandhi personally went around the villages of India speaking to the poor electors and asked them what they had achieved from Shining India. Even though development improves the lives of a common man in the long run, it takes a lot of time and does not show results immediately. This theme, therefore, struck with the people and they gave Congress a good victory. Another thing she did was that in any State where there was a strong regional party, she made an alliance with it and ultimately UPA-I government was formed in 2004. She very wisely decided not to become the prime minister. If she had taken up the position, she would have miserably failed because she had no experience of running governments and no understanding of administration. It was, therefore, a very wise step for her to hold the power from behind the scenes. So she put a non-entity in the front, but a very clever economist, a man with an impeccable image of honesty and integrity—Dr Manmohan Singh. She probably thought that the Sikh community had got alienated from the Congress and having the first Sikh Prime Minister might satisfy the Sikh community, which it did not, but she was able to win the election and the NDA–BJP was shocked with the results.

Now, she has decided that the chain of this dynasty should go into the hands of her son, Rahul Gandhi. She has two children, Rahul Gandhi and Priyanka Gandhi. Priyanka is a very attractive and soft-spoken girl. It is almost universally accepted that she is a better campaigner than Rahul, but the mentality of preferring the son over the daughter is also just as universal. She does not want the mantle to go to her daughter. Rather Sonia Gandhi is very keen that the prime ministership and leadership of the Congress should go to her son, Rahul. She has been trying to build Rahul's image particularly in the last five State elections in India, including Uttar Pradesh, which is the biggest and most populous State in India. Rahul Gandhi had campaigned in all the States very vigorously, thinking that he would be able to make a dent and improve the Congress position. He had enlisted the support of a large number of young people in the Congress, but ultimately when the results came they were shocking for the Congress. The party has fared so poorly, in all the five States that it seems that political future is totally bleak.

Some people even felt that if they had put Priyanka forward, things might have been different. Priyanka was given the charge of two parliamentary constituencies which consisted of ten Assembly constituencies in Uttar Pradesh—one was Rahul Gandhi's parliamentary constituency i.e. Amethi, and the other Sonia Gandhi's parliamentary constituency i.e. Rae Bareli. Both of these constituencies have five Assembly constituencies. Since the assembly elections were going on, the charge of campaigning in these ten constituencies was given to Priyanka. The media showed her spreading charm all around and the Congress was very hopeful. In fact, she had promised to her mother that all ten seats would be won by the Congress. When the results came in, only two seats went to the Congress; it lost eight seats in the strongholds of the Nehru–Gandhi dynasty and in many of those seats, the Congress did not even come second, it came third and sometimes even fourth. Any hopes from Priyanka were also lost and, as far as I can see, this is the end of the road for the family.

12

THE UNDELIVERED LETTER WHICH RESULTED IN THE DECLARATION OF EMERGENCY IN INDIA IN JUNE 1975

It is well-known that the declaration of the Emergency was a black chapter in the political history of this country in which a large number of people had to unnecessarily suffer arbitrary arrest and compulsory sterilization without any redress in the courts. The result of the Emergency created so much hatred among the people of North India that the Congress lost the 1977 general election miserably. In the whole of North India, out of about 350 seats, they were able to win just one—leading to the first non-Congress government coming to power at the Centre.

Generally, people used to put the responsibility for the Emergency on Justice Jagmohanlal Sinha who set aside the election of Indira Gandhi and disqualified her for six years, or myself, who had argued the case against her. But, it was revealed later that it was neither of us, but her own counsel, S.C. Khare, the uncle of a former CJI, Justice V.N. Khare, who was responsible for the Emergency. How this revelation came about, I am setting out hereafter. The following paragraph is from my book, *Courting Destiny:*[7]

> ...in the beginning Mrs Gandhi was being represented by
> the former advocate general of U.P Kanhaiya Lal Misra. By
> the time the evidence came to be recorded in 1975, due
> to Misra's failing health, the case was being conducted by
> Satish Chand Khare, the senior counsel. I am certain that
> if Misra had been advising her in 1975, he would never
> have permitted her to stand in the witness box and we
> should never have had a chance to prove her guilty. It was
> only on the advice of Satish Chand Khare that Mrs Gandhi
> decided to come to the witness box. Khare felt that if such a
> powerful prime minister decided to appear before a junior
> judge of a high court, he would be so overwhelmed by her
> presence that he would not have the courage to decide
> a case against her. I must say that in advising so, Khare
> misjudged Justice Sinha, who was not only a very able and
> hardworking judge, but possessed tremendous courage of
> conviction.

I had written the above in my memoirs, only on my assessment
of Sri Kanhaiya Lal Misra's ability as an accomplished trial lawyer.
After the book was released in November 2008, a lawyer, Mangla
Prasad Bajpai, who had been practising as an advocate in the
Allahabad High Court in 1975, and who was also a junior of Sri
Kanhaiya Lal Misra, read my book in the USA, where he has
been living with his son for many years. He rang me up from
there to tell me that what I had conjectured in my book was in
fact true and that on the very day on which Mrs Gandhi was
to appear in the witness box, Sri Kanhaiya Lal Misra had sent
a letter to her in the morning via his youngest son but he was
not allowed to meet her and the letter remained undelivered.

---

[7]Bhushan, Shanti, *Courting Destiny: A Memoir*, Penguin Books, 2008.

He had written to her not to make the mistake of appearing in the witness box and that even at this eleventh hour she should make some excuse for not appearing. I then asked Mangla Prasad Bajpai to put down these facts in a letter to me.

Shri Bajpai sent me a letter to that effect stating:

> I may state here that I happened to be at the residence of my reverend guru, Mr Kanhaiya Lal Mishra in the morning on the day when Mrs. Gandhi was to appear in the witness box. Finding that Mrs. Gandhi had come to Allahabad for appearing in the court, he addressed a letter to her wherein he emphatically advised her not to appear in the court and excuse herself on one pretext or other. This letter was sent to her through his youngest son Munnan. But as luck would have it, Munnan was not permitted to meet her and she appeared in the witness box. The rest is history.

On 29 January 2009, I sent a letter to Justice A.P. Misra (former Supreme Court judge), son of Pt. Kanhaiya Lal Misra, enclosing a copy of the letter of Sri Mangla Prasad Bajpai to confirm whether the facts stated by Sri Bajpai were true as this was likely to be of historical importance.

I got a reply from Justice A.P. Misra dated 4 February 2009, stating as below:

> As desired by you, I confirm the facts stated in the last para of Mr. Bajpai's letter. In fact the letter which was sent to Mrs. Gandhi, as referred therein, was dictated to me, in which he clearly stated that I am of the clear view, you should not be produced in the witness box. This is a mistake I feel. In addition in this case petitioner himself has not come in the witness box.

Thus it is now clear that it was because the youngest son of Sri Kanhaiya Lal Misra was not allowed to meet Mrs Gandhi and hand over the letter of Shri Misra to her that she appeared as witness and lost the election case. This culminated in the fateful Emergency of 1975. A single mistake by Satish Chand Khare was responsible for the unimaginable distress to lakhs of Indians during the Emergency—an event which nearly brought an end to democracy in the country.

13

THE MAKING OF *JUGNI*

My memoirs have dealt only with my life and the events in it. However, any significant achievement by one's children has to be recorded as an important event of one's own life as well.

On 22 January 2016, my daughter Shefali Bhushan's first Hindi feature film, which was a musical, was released in more than a 100 theatres across the country. The film contains songs sung by illustrious musicians as A.R. Rehman, Vishal Bhardwaj, Rekha Bhardwaj, a Pakistani singer of repute, Bashir, and an acclaimed Qawali singer of Pakistan, Rahat Fateh Ali Khan.

An album of its music had already been released in November of the previous year, in a glittering function held in a theatre in Mumbai and was attended by both A.R. Rehman and Vishal Bhardwaj, who also spoke at the function.

While its pre-release viewing was meant only for film critics and other people connected with films, it received rave reviews. However, the theatres where the film was released on 22 January 2016 had very few viewers because of absolute lack of publicity. The present formula for box office success of a film consists in having a known star and a big budget for promotions running into several crores to attract an audience, at least in the first week.

As new releases are always are on a Friday, all theatres get full on that Friday, and the following Saturday and Sunday—generating an income that is enough to pay not only for the making of the film, including the star's or stars' fees, but also covering the cost of the publicity budget. After that, it does not matter whether the audience likes the film or not because the producers have already recovered their costs and made at least a modest profit. If the film happens to be good, it may continue for several weeks.

This is an aspect of film-making which needs consideration as to how this scenario can be changed. I am told that many excellent films which are made without known stars and without a publicity budget do not get released after being fully shot and edited. This new trend has emerged after the growth of multiplexes in which the film tickets are priced quite high. Today, a ticket in a multiplex may cost about ₹350, whereas when we were young the costliest ticket for the highest class used to be ₹1 in the best of theatres.

Today, there are film-makers who are willing to experiment with new themes and make artistic films. They are highly motivated and sensitive people who produce excellent films. Those interested in such films need to think how this system can be changed so that good films continue to be made and shown in our theatres.

Before I deal with the subject of this chapter, I wish to reiterate that my life essentially consisted of law and politics which have always marched hand in hand. The entire freedom movement in India was led mostly by successful lawyers like Mahatma Gandhi, Motilal Nehru, Jawaharlal Nehru, Dr Rajendra Prasad, and dozens of other leaders.

My own encounter with films has been fairly meagre and has been confined to watching only good films. I started watching films in 1935 or so—when I was less than ten years old—because my father believed in taking his children along when he went to see a film. I remember the earliest films which I saw were *Samudra Manthan, Achhut Kanya* of Bombay Talkies, and *Devdas* of New Theatres. All these were excellent films in their own way.

Adolescent boys in those days used to develop a great fancy for pretty heroines in the films, even to the extent that two of my own close friends at the age of fourteen or fifteen, stole some money from their parents and ran away to Calcutta with the desire to join New Theatres and work with glamorous heroines. It is a different matter that they were not even allowed to enter the gates of New Theatres and had to find employment with some halwai to clean his tables to survive in Calcutta for a few weeks till they came to the conclusion that they had had enough of films and returned to their homes.

There is, however, some similarity between the legal profession and that of film stars. In 2015, one Indu Bhan had written a book, *Legal Eagles*, in which she had written about the exploits of famous Supreme Court lawyers. The seven lawyers selected by her were Harish Salve, Rohinton Nariman, Mukul Rohatgi, Abhishek Singhvi, Arvind Datar, C.A. Sundaram, and Prashant Bhushan. She asked me to write a short foreword for that book which I reproduce below:

> The legal profession is not less glamorous than that of film stars. From time to time, it throws up stars and also some superstars.
>
> The stories of some of these stars and superstars chosen by Indu Bhan for her book provide as fascinating a reading as would a book on Dilip Kumar, Rajesh Khanna and Amitabh Bachchan.
>
> Their exploits which earned them their fame and also their short comings, if any, both have been beautifully covered in this excellent book.

This book will surely be a 'must read book' for all lawyers and also perhaps for some discerning film stars.

In retrospect, it seems that my daughter, Shefali, since childhood was made for the film world. As a young girl, while studying in Modern School, Barakhamba Road, New Delhi, she had acted in a play called *Hirani Kashyap's Murder*, playing the role of a prosecuting counsel. Then again in March 1990, when she was only eighteen years old, she acted in the production of *A Street Car Named Desire* by Tennessee Williams. *The Statesman* of 6 March 1990 published a review with the caption 'Fitting Homage to Williams'. The review said:

> Dramatech is a theatre group with a long history of presenting good serious theatre on the Delhi stage. On Saturday evening they presented the old American classic *A Streetcar Named Desire* by one of the all-time great dramatists Tennessee Williams. This play marked one of the important moments in American Theatre and is considered a landmark. Saturday evening's presentation was directed by Sanjiv Agarwal and he did a creditable job by any standards.
>
> The play was propped by a superb performance by Shefali Bhushan as the nervous and flighty Blanche, the role was wonderfully played without the slightest hint of overplaying. The selection of music was excellent. For all followers of English theatre the play is a must see.

This appreciation obviously encouraged Shefali not only to join a prominent theatre group in Delhi known by the name Act One; but also to join a three-year course of mass communication in Jamia Millia Islamia University, which is one of the finest courses. When Rita Bakhi, a well-known TV film producer watched her performance on the sets of Act One, she was impressed and offered her a role in her TV serial, *Firdous*, a nineteen-episode serial dealing with militancy in Kashmir. In her theatre group, Shefali performed leading roles against actors like Manoj Bajpai and Piyush Mishra. In Jamia, she was the classmate of the well-known TV journalist, Barkha Dutt, both of whom were very close friends. Later, Barkha opted for journalism, while Shefali opted for film-making.

Shefali, from childhood, has been keenly interested in vocal music having had training in classical music. She was greatly influenced by the folk music of India and started finding out about the folk musicians in different corners of India. She adopted the technique of reaching them in their own villages and small towns and recording their music at their own places and putting them on her website, beatofindia.com. She would then make CDs of this folk music in her own studio at Jangpura and sell them and pay 10 per cent royalty to the musicians. This not only helped those musicians in getting an all-India platform for their craft but also helped them make money through their music.

It was through this website that Shefali came in touch with A.R. Rehman, who introduced her to a some film-makers in Mumbai. This is how her venture into film-making began.

When she had completed the script of *Jugni*, Shefali decided to make the film almost on her own. Through A.R. Rehman, she also came in touch with Karan Grover in the film industry. She also came in contact with Manas Malhotra. The three of them got together and decided to make a film with their own investments and formed a partnership under the name Dhun Productions.

The budget of their film could not afford famous stars and so they cast youngsters who were at that time either totally unknown or known very little and could be hired at a reasonable rate. They also got in touch with Clinton Cerejo, a very talented music director, who came along since it was a musical which also had the presence of A.R. Rehman. They also brought along

Shellee, a talented lyricist. They also procured the services of an excellent camera person from Bollywood.

Together they made a very talented team and were thus able to come up with a very beautiful film with great music. The difficulties they encountered during the almost month-long shoot in a village in Punjab have been described by Shefali in a blog she had written about those issues. This, I find, will be quite educative to those youngsters who might be interested in film-making. Her blog titled 'A Film Director's Travels and Travails: The Journey of a First Film' is very interesting and can be easily found on the Internet by googling Shefali Bhushan movie blog.

Deccan Chronicle published a very positive review of *Jugni* in which the author of the review Suparna Sharma said that Shefali Bhushan's *Jugni* was powered by that 'free-spirited feminine energy'.[8]

The *Livemint* review of the film described it as 'an energetic, enjoyable film about the making of music and the unmaking of relationships'.[9] It also said, 'It is nice to walk into an unheralded film and come out keen to recommend it to everyone.' It further added, 'The film's visual aesthetic matches its plain-spoken emotional tenor. Most of it was shot on location in a village called Hassanpur, and Divakar Mani's unfussy, observant camerawork brings out the details very nicely. The writing—screenplay by Bhushan, dialogue by Shellee—is hilariously salty in places; I particularly enjoyed Preeto's assertion to Mastana that she had "X-rayed that chudail" when she first laid eyes on her big-city rival. Clinton Cerejo's soundtrack is the right mix of Punjabi folk,

---

[8]Sharma, Suparna, 'Movie Review Jugni: Hitting some very high notes', *Deccan Chronicle*, 23 January 2016, https://www.deccanchronicle.com/movie-reviews/230116/movie-review-jugni-hitting-some-very-high-notes.html
[9]Bhatia, Uday, 'Film Review: Jugni', *Livemint*, 23 January 2016, https://www.livemint.com/Leisure/emgCPNqoeyRo9OOyIHPCIM/Film-Review-Jugni.html

Sufi and mainstream ballad.'

Another review in *Mumbai Mirror* by Kunal Guha states:

> For a film that revolves around music, Clinton Cerejo puts together a fine collection of traditional Sufi, soul and folk numbers that flow into the ear canals to envelope one in musical ecstasy. Despite being dominated by classical numbers, the soul stirring 'Dugg Duggi Dugg' sung by Vishal Bhardwaj, is a mood number that occupies the mind and heart instantly. Cinematographer Divakar Mani captures the many hues of Punjab like few have. Ditching the state's standard establishing shot: manicured mustard fields, Mani takes us through path – lined by trees devoid of leaves, fog-dusted fields and turquoise blue lakes, some of which cannot resemble Tolkien's world.

I have almost spent seven decades in the legal profession. I recently read somewhere that many lawyers doing the same thing day in and day out get rusted and start thinking of changing over to other vocations. It occurs to me whether at this stage of my life, I can also think of making a career by becoming a film actor. In any case, I would recommend it to other colleagues to think about this kind of change of profession.

I wanted to find out whether anybody in India who had studied law ever became a film actor. I could only find one such person i.e. Kareena Kapoor, who had ventured to study law at Government Law College, Mumbai and could have made a fine lawyer, but she rightly decided to join a more glamorous profession and is one of the top heroines in Bollywood today. Her great-grandfather, Prithvi Raj Kapoor, had studied B.A. from Edward College, Peshawar and then studied law for a year as well; but his heart had been in theatre too.

However, in the West there are plenty of people who studied law but later became successful actors. For example, John Cleese studied Law at Cambridge University and was the founding member of the immensely influential comedy troupe 'Beyond the Fringe', the late Ross Martin graduated from George Washington University School of Law, John Davis Lodge was also a law graduate from Harvard University.

Just as film actors have to deliver their dialogues, lawyers also have to deliver their dialogues to judges. Many of them take great pains in preparing their delivery. I am told, some distinguished lawyers practise the speech that they are going to make in courts before a mirror many times over.

So, let us not lose hope, and continue to believe in ourselves, particularly in our ability to become successful film actors and beat people like Amitabh Bachchan, who have held their stage for too long. Let him and the likes of him face competition now!

14

JUSTICE V.R. KRISHNA IYER:
A JUDICIAL ICON

There have been many great Indian judges in India even during the British rule, like Justice Mehmool in the Allahabad High Court and Justice Muthuswami Aiyyar in the Madras High Court who were great scholars and wrote excellent judgements. Both attained fame during the same period. However, they are not regarded as judicial icons.

After the departure of the British, India has produced many great judges during the last seventy years—but one name which clearly stands out and can be said to have achieved iconic status is Krishna Iyer's.

I have been a great admirer of Krishna Iyer, and I thought I would be failing in my duty if I did not pay tribute to his memory in this book of mine by including a chapter on the greatest judge of our times.

Krishna Iyer was born on 13 November 1915 in a Tamil Brahmin family in Palakkad, Kerala, and entered his 100th year in November 2014. He, however, could not complete 100 years, and died in the first week of December 2014.

Justice Krishna Iyer came to the Supreme Court in 1973 and remained there for a little over seven years. He was not a very senior judge in the Kerala High Court and, had the principle of seniority, which is being applied today, been the criterion in 1973, he would probably not have reached the Supreme Court at all and the country's judiciary would not have attained great heights. He almost single-handedly transformed the Indian jurisprudence and interpreted the Constitution to advance the cause of the poor and deprived sections of our society. He was a great thinker, an eminent scholar, a very hard-working person and, more importantly, a person whose heart kept beating for the cause of the downtrodden. He not only invented new principles but also new expressions in the English language which could bring to life a situation in his judgement.

Justice Krishna Iyer became well-known in the country for the first time in 1975 when, during the summer vacation at the Supreme Court, he heard Palkiwala and me in Mrs Indira Gandhi's stay application against the Allahabad High Court judgement. While Palkiwala was fervently pleading for an unconditional stay in Mrs Gandhi's favour, I was arguing for a complete denial of the stay. He heard both of us very patiently for the whole day and passed his orders the next day. His orders declined an absolute stay to Mrs Gandhi, but granted her a conditional stay so that she could continue as Prime Minister without having a right to vote in the House, thus curbing her prime ministership to a great extent. It was this order which soon thereafter led to the declaration of the Emergency. Janata Party came into existence during the Emergency and formed the first non-Congress government at the Centre, in 1977.

While the legal circles may be familiar with the names of judges of the Supreme Court and some eminent judges of different High Courts, the people in general hardly know the names of even able Supreme Court judges. Justice Krishna Iyer became a household name on account of his having passed a crucial order as a vacation judge in Prime Minister Indira Gandhi's case, which ultimately created history.

It was during the years thereafter that he gave a large number of path-breaking judgements which demonstrated his originality and scholarship. His judgements were not theoretical. He, in fact, visualized practical problems and found judicial solutions to those problems of the poor and the underprivileged.

When Krishna Iyer died, the eminent jurist Fali Nariman said:

> Some judges are compared to tall oak trees—but it is only the tallest oaks, like a Denning in the UK, or a Krishna Iyer in India—who can indulge even with some success in that delicate and unpredictable exercise: of laying down the law in accordance with justice.

Even after his retirement, Krishna Iyer was accessible to people aggrieved and pained, looking for a helping hand. He often described his house in Matthew Arnold's words: 'Home of lost causes, and forsaken beliefs, and unpopular names, and impossible loyalties.'

Krishna Iyer will be remembered as a constructive legislator, prolific speaker, forceful crusader, copious writer, and an excellent human being whose jurisprudence breathed new life into what was seen as a listless institution and made the Supreme Court the most powerful institution of its kind in the world, by redesigning constitutional remedies to address constitutional aberrations.

I will start with a few quotes from Krishna Iyer himself. He had stated that, 'Our legal system, including the police, is anti-Dalit and anti-poor. The death penalty laws' wrathful majesty, in blood-shot equality, deals the fatal blow on the poor not the rich, the pariah not the Brahmin, the black not the white, the underdog not the top dog, the dissenter not the conformist.

The law barks at all but bites only the poor, the powerless, the illiterate, the ignorant.' He also said, 'Law is not a trade, not briefs, but merchandise, and so the heaven of commercial competition should not vulgarize the legal profession.'

In an important judgement in 1975, he had said, 'The mortality of justice at the hands of law troubles a judge's conscience and points an angry interrogation at the law reformer. The humanist rule that procedure should be the handmaid, not the mistress, of legal justice compels consideration of vesting a residuary power in judges to act ex debito justitiae where the tragic sequel otherwise would be wholly inequitable. Justice is the goal of jurisprudence.'

I have selected just three of Krishna Iyer's judgements which speak eloquently about his jurisprudence. Coincidentally, all the three judgements are from what I regard as the golden period of Indian jurisprudence, a period when the Janata Party Government was in power at the Centre—from 1977 to 1979.

In Nandini Satpathy's case, decided in 1978, Krishna Iyer was dealing with the problem of police interrogation and he read the 'right to silence' in Article 20(3) of the Constitution. He referred to the paradox in the words of Lewis Mayers: 'To strike the balance between the needs of law enforcement on the one hand and the protection of the citizen from oppression and injustice at the hands of the law-enforcement machinery on the other is a perennial problem of statecraft.' He explained the spirit behind the developing concept of 'right to silence' and reading the same in Article 20(3) of the Constitution in the following words:

> Whether we consider the Talmudic law or the Magna Carta, the Fifth Amendment, the provisions of other constitutions or Article 20(3), the driving force behind the refusal to permit forced self-crimination is the system of torture by investigators and courts from medieval times to

modern days. Law is a response to life and the English rule of the accused's privilege of silence may easily be traced as a sharp reaction to the Court of Star Chamber when self-incrimination was not regarded as wrongful. Indeed, then the central feature of the criminal proceedings, as Holdsworth has noted, was the examination of the accused.

The horror and terror that then prevailed did, as a reaction, give rise to the reverential principle of immunity from interrogation for the accused. Sir James Stephen has observed:

> For at least a century and a half the (English) Courts have acted upon the supposition that to question a prisoner is illegal. This opinion arose from a peculiar and accidental state of things which has long since passed away and our modern law is in fact derived from somewhat questionable source though it may no doubt be defended.

Many police officers, Indian and foreign, may be perfect gentlemen, many police stations, here and elsewhere, may be wholesome. Even so, the law is made for the generality and Gresham's Law does not spare the police force.

Therefore, 'third degree' has to be outlawed and indeed has been. We have to draw up clear lines between the whirlpool and the rock where the safety of society and the worth of the human person may coexist in peace.

He referred to the American judgement in Miranda case by saying, 'The Miranda ruling clothed the Fifth Amendment with flesh and blood and so must we, if Article 20(3) is not to prove a promise of unreality.' After quoting copiously from the US judgement in the Miranda case, he said, 'We feel that by successful interpretation judge-centred law must catalyse community-centred legality.'

He added:

> There is one touch of nature which makes the judicial world kin—the love of justice-in-action and concern for human values. So, regardless of historical origins and political borrowings, the framers of our Constitution have cognised certain pessimistic poignancies and mellow life meanings and obligated judges to maintain a 'fair state-individual balance' and to broaden the fundamental right to fulfil its purpose, lest frequent martyrdoms reduce the article to a mock formula. Even silent approaches, furtive moves, slight deviations and subtle ingenuities may erode the article's validity unless the law outlaws illegitimate and unconstitutional procedures before they find their first firm footing. The silent cause of the final fall of the tall tower is the first stone obliquely and obliviously removed from the base. And Article 20(3) is a human article, a guarantee of dignity and integrity and of inviolability of the person and refusal to convert an adversary system into an inquisitorial scheme in the antagonistic ante-chamber of a police station.

He finally recorded his views in the following terms:

> We hold that Section 161 enables the police to examine the accused during investigation. The prohibitive sweep of Article 20(3) goes back to the stage of police interrogation—not, as contended, commencing in court only. In our judgment, the provisions of Article 20(3) and Section 161(1) substantially cover the same area, so far as police investigations are concerned. The ban on self-accusation and the right to silence, while one investigation or trial is under way, goes beyond that case and protects the accused in regard to other offences pending or imminent.

As a visionary, he indicated as to what kind of police force was needed for our Republic. In his own words:

The Indian Republic cannot fulfil its social justice tryst without a serious strategy of cultural and organizational transformation of police intelligence and investigation, abjuring fists and emphasizing wits, setting apart a separate, sophisticated force with special skills, drills, techniques and technology and aloof from the fossilising, sometimes marginally feudal, assignments—like V.I.P duty, sentry duty, traffic duty, law and order functions, border security operations. They must develop an ethos and ethic and professionalism and probity which can effectively meet the challenge of criminal cunning, the menace of macabre intricacies and the subtle machinations of white-collar criminals in politics, business and professions and can do so without resort to vulgarity, violence or other vice. The methods, manners and morals of the police force are the measure of a society's cultural tolerance and a government's real refinement.

I feel all police officers in the country as well as the bureaucrats need to read this carefully and try their best to reform the investigating police in the country as Justice Krishna Iyer had envisaged in this judgement.

In the case of M.H. Hoskot vs State of Maharashtra, also decided in 1978, Justice Krishna Iyer had to interpret Article 21. It states that, 'No person shall be deprived of his life or personal liberty except according to the procedure established by law.' According to the State, it had only to comply with the written text of the letter in order to deprive a person of his life and liberty. This argument was possible and had earlier been accepted in the Supreme Court also because the Constituent Assembly had not adopted the due process clause from the American Constitution. However, Justice Krishna Iyer dealt with the problem in the following words:

'Procedure established by law' are words of deep meaning for all lovers of liberty and judicial sentinels. Amplified, activist fashion 'procedure' means 'fair and reasonable procedure' which comports with civilised norms like natural justice rooted firm in community consciousness— not primitive processual barbarity nor legislated normative mockery.

The facts which gave rise to the case were put by Justice Krishna Iyer in the following words:

> The facts, more flabbergasting than fantasy, present themselves in this Special Leave Petition. The appeal is against a conviction concurrently rendered for a novel and daring set of crimes and follow-up sentence of three-year prison term. The offence is bizarre, the offender perplexing, the sentence incredibly indiscreet at the Sessions Court stage but reasonably just at the High Court level and, to cap it all, the delay in seeking leave from this Court doubly shocking because it is inordinate and implicates the prison administration.

The Petitioner was a Reader in the Saurashtra University, a PhD from Karnataka University, and in his case the High Court judgement was pronounced in November 1973 but the Special Leave Petition had been made well over four years later. This hiatus may appear horrendous, all the more so because the petitioner had undergone his full term of imprisonment during this lengthy interregnum. The petitioner had explained the reason for the delay in his application for condonation of delay which disclosed a disturbing episode of prison injustice, according to Krishna Iyer's judgement. It was this which led to the directions given in the judgement of Justice Krishna Iyer requiring the courts to furnish a free transcript of the judgement when sentencing a person to a prison term. And where the prisoner sought to file an appeal or revision, every facility for exercise of that right shall be made available by the jail administration. More importantly, where a prisoner was disabled from engaging a lawyer, on account of indigence or an incommunicado situation, the court shall assign competent counsel for the prisoner's defence.

It was Justice Krishna Iyer's strong belief that the powers conferred on the courts should be exercised suo moto when the ends of justice so demanded, and did not require even the affected person to approach the court. He was even willing to accept a postcard as a Writ Petition and initiate action thereon if the interests of justice so demanded. The court was in a position to secure facts from the State and necessary directions could be given by the court to the various authorities.

The case of Sunil Batra and Charles Sobhraj, one Indian and the other a French citizen, the Indian being charged with the offence of murder and the French facing grave charges, also required going into prison justice. In the words of Justice Krishna Iyer:

> The province of prison justice, the conceptualization of freedom behind bars and the role of judicial power as constitutional sentinel in a prison setting, are of the gravest moment in a world of escalating torture by the minions of State, and in India, where this virgin area of jurisprudence is becoming painfully relevant.

He pithily put the question arising out of the case in the following terms:

> One important interrogation lies at the root of these twin writ petitions: Does a prison setting, ipso facto, out-law the rule of law, lock out the judicial process from the jail gates

and declare a long holiday for human rights of convicts in confinement, and (to change the metaphor) if there is no total eclipse, what luscent segment is open for judicial justice?

He explained his philosophy in the following terms:

I may now crystallise this legal discussion. Disciplinary autonomy, in the hands of mayhem-happy jail staffers, may harry human rights and the wails from behind the high walls will not easily break through the sound-proof, sight-proof barrier to awaken the judges' writ jurisdiction. So, it follows that activist legal aid as a pipeline to carry to the court the breaches of prisoners' basic rights is a radical humanist concomitant of the rule of prison law. And in our constitutional order it is axiomatic that the prison laws do not swallow up the fundamental rights of the legally unfree, and, as sentinels on the qui-vive, courts will guard freedom behind bars, tempered, of course, by environmental realism but intolerant of torture by executive echelons. The policy of the law and the paramountcy of the Constitution are beyond purchase by authoritarians glibly invoking 'dangerousness' of inmates and peace in prisons.

He referred to community-based litigation and participative justice, supportive of democratic legality, in the following words:

A few special forensic features of the proceedings before us have seminal significance. I advert to them in limine as helpful factors in the progressive development of the legal process.

The essence of this class of litigation is not adjudication on particular grievances of individual prisoners but broad delivery of social justice. It goes beyond mere moral weight-lifting or case-by-case correction but transcends into forensic humanisation of a harsh legal legacy which has for long hidden from judicial view. It is the necessitous task of this Court, when invited appropriately, to adventure even into fresh areas of agony and injustice and to inject humane constitutional ethic into imperial statutory survivals, especially when the (prison) Executive, thirty years after Independence defends the alleged wrong as right and the Legislatures, whose members, over the decades, are not altogether strangers to the hurtful features of jails, are perhaps pre-occupied with more popular business than concern for the detained derelicts who are a scattered, voiceless, noiseless minority.

Justice Krishna Iyer, for this reason, allowed Citizens for Democracy, an organization operating in the field of human rights, to intervene in Sobhraj's case, and on behalf of that organization, Shri Tarkunde made legal submissions fuelled by passion for jail reforms. Justice Krishna Iyer also explained his judicial strategy of not striking down legislation, but when necessary interpreting it in such a manner as to achieve what was required. He said:

But, the Court does not 'rush in' to demolish provisions where judicial endeavour, amelioratively interpretational, may achieve both constitutionality and compassionate resurrection. This salutary strategy of sustaining the validity of the law and softening its application was, with lovely dexterity, adopted by Sri Soli Sorabjee appearing for the State. The semantic technique of updating the living sense of a dated legislation is, in our view, perfectly legitimate, especially when, in a developing country like ours, the corpus juris is, in some measure a Raj hangover.

He added:

To meet the needs of India today, the imperatives of Independence desiderate a creative role for the Courts in interpretation and application, specially when enactments from the imperial mint govern. Words grow with the world. That is the dynamics of semantics.

He further explained:

> The jurisprudence of statutory construction, especially when a vigorous break with the past and smooth reconciliation with a radical constitutional value-set are the object, uses the art of reading down and reading wide, as part of interpretational engineering.

Justice Krishna Iyer and his colleagues on the bench decided in that case to personally inspect the Tihar Prison, so that they could make recommendations in respect of prison justice.

Justice Iyer was a very well-read person, and in this case, he quoted from Charles Dickens' *American Notes and Pictures from Italy*, which had referred to the cruelty of 'solitary confinement' in a Pennsylvania Penitentiary. He also referred to Oscar Wilde and quoted Jawaharlal Nehru from his autobiography. After a very long discussion, he concluded:

> Sobhraj, in chains, demands constitutional rights for man. For there are several men like him in the same prison, under trials, indigents, even minors! The official journal allegedly registers the laconic reason for the Jail Superintendent's fiat to impose bar fetters and these 'dangerous' reasons are recorded in English in the history tickets of the (mostly) 'C' class 'un-English' victims. This voodoo is in compliance with the formula of the rule and jail visitors' march past. The Inspector-General of Prisons revises, if moved, and the spirit-crushing artifice survives as a technique of jail discipline. Ordinarily, the curtain falls, the groan of moan is hardly heard, the world falls to sleep, the Constitution and the Court sublimely uphold human

rights but the cells weep for justice unheard.

He also said, 'The great problems of law are the grave crises of life and both can be solved not by the literal instruction of printed enactments, but by the interpretative sensitization of the heart to "the still, sad, music of humanity".

He finally recorded his conclusion in the following terms:

> I hold that bar fetters are a barbarity generally and, like whipping, must vanish. Civilised consciousness is hostile to torture within the walled campus. We hold that solitary confinement, cellular segregation and marginally modified editions of the same process are inhuman and irrational. More dangerous are these expedients when imposed by the unturned and untrained power of a jail superior who has, as part of his professional equipment, no course in human psychology, stressology or physiology, who has to depend on no medical or psychiatric examination prior to infliction of irons or solitary, who has no obligation to hear the victim before harming him, whose 'reasons' are in English on the history-tickets and therefore unknowable and in the Journal to which the prisoner has no access.

The above mentioned judgements demonstrate the judicial originality, scholarship, and humanism of Justice Krishna Iyer's judicial philosophy. It is this contribution which makes him a judicial icon that is almost impossible to replicate.

15

THE CASE OF KAMAKHYA TEMPLE

For many centuries, the Brahmin communities have found ingenious ways to exploit the religious sentiments of the Indian public. They have created huge temples, invented and spread interesting myths around those temples and their deities, and created a belief among the credulous public that the deities in those temples are so powerful that they can fulfil any desire of a devotee who worships there with deep reverence as instructed by the Brahmin priests. All the Hindu temples in India are kept under the management of the Brahmin community. A complex set of rituals has also been devised by them from temple to temple to convince simple folks into believing that these rituals have great efficacy and they are a shortcut to prosperity and happiness in one's life. This is the reason that these temples continuously receive huge funds which, of course, normally benefit the Brahmin priests working in those temples.

The Kamakhya Temple is a famous pilgrimage site situated in Guwahati, Assam. The temple is located on the Nilachal Hill in Guwahati at about 8 kms from the railway station. It is dedicated to tantric goddesses. Apart from the deity Kamakhya Devi, the compound of the temple houses ten other avatars of Kali namely, Dhumavati, Matangi, Bagola, Tara, Kamala, Bhairavi,

Chinnamasta, Bhuvaneshwari, and Tripura Sundari.

Mythical History

The temple of Kamakhya has a very interesting story of its origin. It is one of the 108 Shakti Peeths. The story of the Shakti Peeths is that once Sati fought with her husband Shiva to attend her father's great yagna. But at the grand yagna, Sati's father Daksha insulted her husband. Sati was enraged and in her shame, she jumped into the fire and killed herself. When Shiva came to know that his beloved wife had committed suicide, he went insane with rage. He placed Sati's dead body on his shoulders and did the tandav—dance of destruction.

To calm him down, Vishnu cut the dead body with his chakra. The 108 places where Sati's body parts fell are called Shakti Peeths. Kamakhya Temple is special because it was Sati's womb and vagina that fell there.

The Name 'Kamakhya'

Kamadeva—the God of love—had lost his virility due to a curse. He sought out Shakti's womb and genitals and was freed from the curse. This is where 'love' gained his potency and thus the deity 'Kamakhya Devi' was installed and worshipped here.

Some people also believe that the Kamakhya Temple is a place where Shiva and Devi Sati had their romantic encounters. As the Sanskrit word for lovemaking is 'kama', the place was named Kamakhya.

The Bleeding Goddess

Kamakhya Devi is known as the bleeding goddess. The mythical womb and vagina of Shakti are supposed to be installed in the 'Garvagriha' or sanctum sanctorum of the temple. In the month of Ashad (June–July), the goddess menstruates. At this time, the Brahmaputra River near Kamakhya turns red. The temple then remains closed for three days and holy water is distributed among the devotees of Kamakhya Devi. There is no scientific proof that it is blood that actually turns the river red. Some people say that the priests pour vermilion into the waters. But symbolically, menstruation is the symbol of a woman's creativity and the power to give birth. So, the deity and the temple of Kamakhya celebrate this 'shakti' or power within every woman.

History of the Kamakhya Temple

Legend has it that Narakasura, the king of Pragjyotishpura, built the Kamakhya Temple in the twelfth century. However, what we find in the recorded history of eighteenth century is that the Ahom Kings, who ruled Assam then, brought many families of Brahmins from northern India (Kanauj) to there. The Bardeuries are understood to comprise five families—the Bhramas, Pujaris or Pujaks, Chandipathaks, Bidhipathaks, and Hotas. The Brahma family has since become extinct.

The Pujaks later somehow got divided into Deka and Bura. In Assamese 'Deka' means the young and 'Bura' means the old.

As the names indicate, the ancestor of each separate group of the Bardeuris was appointed to perform a special function in the scheme of conducting worship, ordinary or special, at the Kamakhya Temple. The Bura and the Deka came from the same stock and originated from a common ancestor. The Bardeuris of these two groups were apparently the persons whose ancestors were appointed to perform the duties of regular priest or Pujaks in the Kamakhya Temple. But the other three families cannot be ignored, and there were three special functions allotted to them in connection to special pujas or ceremonies. The Bidhipathak, as the name indicates, were to attend all important puja or worship with their 'Bidhi' (the book of rituals and procedures) and to guide the officiating priest properly in conducting worship and performing the details of the technique and leading him to say the mantras correctly and accurately. The Hota is to perform 'Homa' or the kindling of the sacred fire in all functions where it is an essential part. The Brahma is to attend all important functions and count the number of offerings given at a Homa, so that the prescribed number is neither reduced nor increased. Thus the Pujak, Bidhipathak, Hota, and Brahma were the four indispensable officials to perform a special or important worship in the Kamakhya temple. The Pujak family having been subdivided into Deka and Bura, they were all collectively known as Panchghar Bordeuri (five families of high priests).

In point of fact, the Ahom kings also brought various other Brahmin families like Supakars, Japaks, Adhikaries, etc., for the performance of various other priestly duties in the principal and subsidiary temples of Kamakhya. Not only this, the Ahom kings brought several other non-Brahmin families like the Asthaprahari (Athparia or security personals), the Duwari (gatekeepers), the Sonari (goldsmiths), the Gayan (singers), the Bayan (musicians), the Bharali (storekeepers), etc.

The head priest of Kamakhya Temple is known as the Doloi and he had full authority over extensive offerings made in the temple. So far as the selection of the Doloi was concerned, the Calcutta High Court in 1940 had gone into the history of selection of the Doloi and powers which the Doloi exercised. Below is what the Calcutta High Court had said:

> The evidence also establishes the fact that during the time
> of the Hindu kings, the male members of these families

had no concern with the secular management, that is to say, the management of the endowed properties; but their duties were confined to the internal affairs of the temple. The Hindu kings or their representatives appointed a man from outside for the purpose of managing the properties of the endowment and exercising general supervision over the persons who were in charge of the worship of the deity. He was called the sebachalac. The aforesaid families are called Bardeoris. The evidence establishes that for the purpose of the smooth working of the ceremonies, the adult male members of the said families appointed or elected from amongst them, one person as the chief to supervise the worship. He is called the Daloi. At the time of the Hindu kings the selection so made had to be sanctioned by the kind or his representative. The question in controversy is whether the man to be selected as Daloi by the Bardeoris, is to be an adult male member of any of the four families, or whether the selection is to be confined to the Bura and the Deka families only. This is the controversy in the appeal which we will have to decide.

We proceed on with the narratives just before the conquest of Assam by the British. The Burmese had overrun the province and in the unsettled state, certain events occurred on which there were proceedings after peace and order had been restored by the British Government. Some of these proceedings have important bearing on the question which we have to decide in the present case. After the British conquest in 1826 it appears that the old system continued up to 1842. In 1842 instructions were issued by the British Government to the effect that the said Government or its officers would have no concern with the affairs of the Kamakhya temple. The result of this declaration of policy of the British Government had a twofold effect. One was that the necessity of obtaining the sanction of the ruling authority or of the State, to the appointment of a Daloi selected by the Bardeoris dropped out. The other the Daloi who was up to that time only concerned with the internal affairs of the temple, acquired the power of managing the properties of the endowment, that is to say, acquired secular powers. These facts which we have recited are borne out by proceedings taken either before the revenue authorities or before the Badar Dewani Adalat.

So, a custom had grown that all the male adult members of the four Brahmin families used to elect a Doloi who had started exercising the power of looking after the properties of the temple including all the offerings received from the various devotees.

Thus, in spite of the fact that the people who were serving in the temple in different capacities included non-Brahmins as well as the women of the four Brahmin families—neither those women nor the functionaries, who were non-Brahmin, had any say in the management of the temple.

It was when a new Doloi had been elected by the male adult members of those four Brahmin families that we filed two Writ Petitions in the Supreme Court where some other controversy relating to the Kamakhya Temple was pending in civil appeal, and challenged the election of the Doloi which had been brought about by the Collector of Guwahati by following the customs. The main ground raised in the two petitions was that after the Constitution had been enacted in 1950, even a custom, which was discriminatory, became void as contravening the fundamental rights enshrined in the Constitution. We relied in this connection, on Article 14 and Article 15(1) which are extracted below:

Article 14: The State shall not deny to any person equality before the law, equal protection of laws within the territory of India.

Article 15(1): The State shall not discriminate against any citizen on ground only on religion, race, caste, sex, place of birth or any of them.

So far as the invalidation of the custom was concerned, for contravention of these fundamental rights, we placed reliance on Article 13, the relevant parts of which are extracted below:

Article 13(1): All laws in force in the territory of India immediately before the commencement of this Constitution, insofar as they are inconsistent with the provisions of this part, shall, to the extent of such inconsistency, be void.

Article 13(3)(a): In this Article, unless the context otherwise requires—

'Law' includes any ordinance, order, bye-law, rule, regulation, notification, custom or usage having in the territory of India shall have the force of law.

Our contention was that since the custom mentioned above regarding election of the Doloi was being recognized by the courts and enforced in the matter of election of the Doloi, a custom which, for no rhyme or reason, excluded the women of even the four Brahmin families and which also excluded the non-Brahmin members serving the temple in different capacities from having any voice in the election of the Doloi, had become unconstitutional and could not survive after the enactment of the Constitution. To this argument of ours, which in my opinion was a very powerful one, the reply from the elected Doloi's side was twofold: (1) that the custom related to the management of a temple, which was covered by Article 26 of the Constitution, another important fundamental right given to every religious denomination. The relevant part of Article 26 is extracted below:

Article 26: Subject to public order, morality and health, every religious denomination or any section there of shall have the right—

2. to establish and maintain institutions for religious and charitable purposes;

3. to manage its own affairs in matters of religion;

It was the contention on behalf of the elected Doloi that the election of the chief priest, namely the Doloi, was a part of fundamental right of the religious denomination which has established the Kamakhya Temple to manage its own affairs in matters of religion and, therefore, this could not be violated by giving a right of vote either to the women or to members of castes other than Brahmins.

The second contention of the elected Doloi was that Articles 14 and 15 only restrained the State from denying equality on the ground of caste or sex but since the custom had not been established by the State, and so merely being recognized by the courts as part of the enforceable law, it could not become void for contravention of Articles 14 or 15.

A seven-judge bench of the Supreme Court in the case of Shri Laxmindra Thirtha Swamiar of Sri Shirur Matt in 1954 SCR 1005 had interpreted Article 26 of the Constitution. It had held that, 'It is clear, therefore, that question merely relating to administration of properties belonging to a religious group or institution are not matters of religion to which clause (b) of the Article applies.'

It, however, also proceeded to hold that, 'Under Article 26(b) therefore, a religious denomination or organization enjoys complete autonomy in the matter of deciding as to what rights and ceremonies are essential according to the tenets of the religion, that no outside authority has any jurisdiction to interfere with their decision in such matters.' It also held that, 'It should be noticed, however, that under Article 26(d), it is the fundamental right of a religious denomination or its representative to administer its properties in accordance with the law, and law, therefore, must leave the right of administration to the religious denomination itself subject to such restrictions and regulations as it might choose to impose. A law which takes away the right of administration from the hands of a religious denomination altogether and vests it in any other authority would amount to violation of the right guaranteed under Clause (d) of Article 26.'

A Constitution Bench consisting of five judges of the Supreme Court had gone to consider the question in the case of Nathdwara Temple in Tilkayat Shri Govindlalji Maharaj vs The State of Rajasthan and Others, had held that:

> The right to manage the properties of a temple was a purely secular matter and it cannot, in our opinion, be regarded as a religious practice so as to fall under Art. 25(1) or as amounting to affairs in matters of religion.

It further observed that it was difficult to accede to the argument that the tenets of the Vallabhi cult require as a matter of religion that the properties must be managed by the Tilkayat. It finally laid down that:

> A distinction must always be made between a practice which is religious and a practice in regard to a matter which is purely secular and has no element of religion associated with it. Therefore, we are satisfied that the claim made by the denomination that the Act impinges on the rights guaranteed to it by Art. 25(1) and 26(b) must be rejected.

In 1996, the Supreme Court in the case of A.S. Narayana Deekshitulu vs State of Andhra Pradesh drew a clear distinction between religious service as such and the person who performed the same. It held that the selection of the person who performed the religious service could not be regarded as part of a religious practice and, therefore, the legislature was competent to take away the hereditary right to succeed to the office of a priest. It further held that the act of appointment of an Archak was a secular matter and a Shebiat or manager to a temple exercised essentially a secular function in choosing and appointing an Archak. It further held that even the religious head of a temple could not claim hereditary rights and, therefore, an abolition of hereditary rights of priests did not violate Article 26(b) of the Constitution. The same view has been taken in several other cases decided by the Supreme Court.

The Supreme Court in our Writ Petitions, therefore, observed as below:

> There is no need to go into all the case laws in respect of Articles 25 and 26 because by now it is well settled that Article 25(2)(a) and Article 26(b) guaranteeing the right to every religious denomination to manage its own affairs in matters of religion are subject to and can be controlled by a law contemplated under Article 25(2)(b) asboth Articles are required to be read harmoniously.

The court, therefore, came to the conclusion that if the legislature had enacted a law to provide that notwithstanding the custom of excluding the families and the non-Brahmins from the electoral college to elect the Doloi, the ultimate head of the temple to manage its properties, the legislature would be competent to do so. However, the court's view was that in the absence of such legislation, the contention that the court could declare the custom to have become unconstitutional after the enactment of the Constitution was not acceptable because the judiciary in its view was not part of the State when it was deciding matters in its judicial spheres. It, therefore, denied relief to us in the following words:

In the aforesaid situation it is always with a heavy heart that a Writ Court has to deny relief. It may not always be safe for a Writ Court to decide issues and facts having great impact on the general public or a large part of it only on the basis of oath against oath. Where the right is admitted and well established, the Writ Court will not hesitate in implementing such a right especially a fundamental right. But enforcement of established rights is a different matter than the establishment of the right itself. When there is a serious dispute between two private parties as to the expertise, experience and qualification for a particular job, the prime task before the Court is first to analyse the facts for coming to a definite conclusion whether the right stands established and only when the answer is in affirmative, the Court may have no difficulty in enforcing such an established right, whether statutory, fundamental or constitutional. In the present case, as indicated above, it is indeed difficult for this Court to come to a definite conclusion that the petitioners claim to equality for the purpose at hand is well established. Hence we have no option but to deny relief to the petitioners.

On the question of applicability of Articles 12, 13, 14, and 15, below is what the Supreme Court said:

On the related issue of the scope of Article 12 and whether for the purposes of issuance of writ, judicial decisions by the judiciary can be included in State action, we are in agreement with the submissions advanced by Mr. Rajiv Dhavan that definition of 'the state' under Article 12 is contextual depending upon all relevant facts including the concerned provisions in Part III of the Constitution. The definition is clearly inclusive and not exhaustive. Hence omission of judiciary when the government and Parliament of India as well as government and legislature of each of the

State has been included is conspicuous but not conclusive that judiciary must be excluded.

It further held that the cases cited by us in regard to the judiciary being part of the State under Articles 12, 13, 14, and 15 and the reliance placed by us on Harjinder Singh vs Punjab State Warehousing Corporation in 2010 (3) SCC 192 and Indira Nehru Gandhi vs Raj Narain in 1975 (Suppl.) SCC 1, those observations are not binding on them.

The Supreme Court Bench thereafter, after dismissing our Writ Petitions, acted proactively in favour of the elected Brahmin Doloi and gave directions to the District Administration in the following terms:

> Since the Debutter Board is occupying some part of the premises in the temple of Sri Sri Maa Kamakhya temple on account of interim orders of this court, all those interim orders are now vacated. The District administration is directed to ensure that those premises are vacated by the members or representatives of the Debutter Board at the earliest and in any case within four weeks. The premises and other properties of Sri Sri Maa Kamakhya Temple shall, if required, be placed back within the same time in possession of the Bordeories Samaj through the last elected Dolois against receipts which shall be retained in the office of Deputy Commissioner, Guwahati. The parties representing the Debutter board are also directed to hand over the vacant and peaceful possession of the concerned premises and other properties of the temple, if any, within four weeks.

I find this proactive action of the court to be quite inconsistent with the observations made earlier that it was with a heavy heart that a Writ Court has to deny relief to the petitioners.

The Supreme Court's decision of 2010, which we relied upon,

made the following very important observations:

> 40. In this context another aspect is of some relevance and it was pointed out by Hidayatullah, J, as His Lordship then was, in Naresh Shridhar Mirajkar v. State of Maharashtra. In a minority judgment, His Lordship held that the judiciary is a State within the meaning of Article 12. (See AIR paras 100 101 at pp.28 and 29 of the Report). This minority view of His Lordship was endorsed by Mathew, J. in Kesavananda Bharati (at SCC p.877, para 1703: AIR p. 1949, para 1717 of the Report) and it was held that the State under Article 12 would include the judiciary. This was again reiterated by Mathew J., in the Constitution Bench judgment in State of Kerala v. N.M. Thomas where Mathew J's view was the majority view, though given separately. At SCC p. 343, para 64: AIR p. 515, para 89 of the Report, His Lordship held that under Article 12, 'State' would include 'Court'.
>
> 41. In view of such an authoritative pronouncement the definition of the State under Article 12 encompass the judiciary and in Kesavananda case it was held that 'judicial process' is also 'State action', (SCC p877, para 1703: AIR p. 1949, para 1717).
>
> 47. Krishna Iyer, J, speaking for the Court, made it very clear (S. Naganatha case, SCC p. 467, para 1) that even though the Judges are 'constitutional invigilators and statutory interpreters' they should also be responsive to Part IV of the Constitution being 'one of the trinity of the nation's appointed instrumentalities in the transformation of the socio-economic order'. The learned Judge made it very clear that when the Judges 'decode social legislation', they 'must be animated by a goal-oriented approach' and the learned Judge opined, and if I may say so, unerringly, that in this country 'the judiciary is not a mere umpire, as some assume, but an activist catalyst in the constitutional

scheme' (SCC p. 468, para 1).

The same view had been taken by the US Supreme Court also in a case reported in 92 L.ed. 1161, Shelley v. Kraemer. In a decision rendered in 1947, the Court had clearly stated:

> That the action of state courts and of judicial officers in their official capacities is to be regarded as action of the State within the meaning of the Fourteenth Amendment, is a proposition which has long been established by decisions of this Court. That principle was given expression in the earliest cases involving the construction of the terms of the Fourteenth Amendment. Thus, in Virginia v. Rives, 100 US 313, 318, 25 L ed 667, 669 (1880), this Court stated: 'It is doubtless true that a State may act through different agencies, either by its legislative, its executive, or its judicial authorities; and the prohibitions of the amendment extend to all action of the State denying equal protection of the laws, whether it be action by one of these agencies or by another'. In Ex parte Virginia, 100 US 339, 347, 25 L ed 676, 679 (1880), the Court observed: 'A State acts by its legislative, its executive, or its judicial authorities. It can act in no other way'. In the Civil Rights Cases, 109 US 3, 11, 17, 27, L ed 835, 839, 841 (1883), this Court pointed out that the Amendment makes void 'State action of every kind' which is inconsistent with the guaranties therein contained, and extends to manifestations of 'State authority in the shape of laws, customs, or judicial or executive proceedings'. Language to like effect is employed no less than eighteen times during the course of that opinion.

When the judgement was delivered, we were a little surprised because in all these years since the Supreme Court had been established in 1950 it has always been taking a very progressive view and has been carrying out a lot of social reforms through its judgements. In fact, we had also referred in our submissions before the bench, and cited an article in which fifteen judgements of the Supreme Court had been mentioned and in which the interest of women had been advanced by the Supreme Court in different eventualities.

It seems it will take some more time for the gender discrimination to be finally ended in India as well as to be completely done away with caste discrimination against lower castes.

It is relevant to note the recent presidential election in the United States of America in which there was a strong attempt and people were very hopeful that the glass ceiling would be shattered by having the first woman president of the US in a very competent Hillary Clinton. Contrary, however, to opinion polls, it seems that male chauvinism prevailed in America also, and Donald Trump, who is evidently unfit to be the US President, got elected by the electoral system. It is remarkable that although overall Hillary Clinton got two lakh votes more than Trump did, but on account of their Electoral College system, Trump prevailed by quite a margin.

I believe that when we established India as a secular country in 1950, religious rights should not have been granted by the State as fundamental rights in the Constitution. However, perhaps the political leaders who were responsible for framing the Constitution rightly wanted at that point in time in history all sections having power and influence in the country to be brought on board in a spirit of compromise and that is why various religious communities were given some fundamental rights. Perhaps it was a wise step at that point in time. Apart from Articles 25 and 26 which had already been referred to, Article 30 also granted a fundamental right to religious minorities to establish and administer educational institutions of their choice.

This also, to my mind, was an effort at a compromise to bring those who were running those institutions on board and to have a Constitution with the consent of all power groups in the country.

However, wisely, by Article 368, power was given to the Parliament to amend the Constitution from time to time. In a case, a thirteen-judge bench of the Supreme Court had found the much-needed exception to this power of amendment that the essential features of the Indian Constitution like secularism, democracy, etc., could not be done away with through the exercise of the power of amendment. However, it is hoped that the power of amendment in Article 368 would be exercised in times to come wisely so that we could have an even better polity and more efficient governance in the country in order to speedily address several problems, particularly of the poor.

16

THE DEMOLITION CASE OF DELHI PARAMEDICAL AND MANAGEMENT INSTITUTE (DPMI)

As is well-known, it is almost impossible to get building plans for the construction of a building sanctioned by the Delhi Municipal Corporation within a reasonable time without bribing the officials concerned.

My family members had purchased three small adjacent plots with an area of 175 square yard each, in a public auction by the Delhi Development Authority (DDA) in Jangpura, New Delhi. After the purchase of these plots, I told my architect to prepare building plans on all the three plots for the maximum built-up area permissible, strictly in accordance with the building regulations. I told him that I wanted to construct the three buildings as soon as possible after the sanction of the building plans. But he explained that it would be impossible to get the plan sanctioned in the foreseeable future unless I was prepared to pay a bribe to the officials concerned. I told him that giving a bribe was not only unethical but also an offence under the Indian Penal Code and, therefore, I could not be a party to the payment of any bribe for getting the plan sanctioned, and if there is delay in the sanction of the plan, I would rather wait before starting construction. The building plans were submitted by the architect to the Municipal Corporation promptly.

For seven years, till the year 2000, the building plans were not sanctioned and, therefore, the construction of the buildings could not start. It seems that the patience of the Municipal authorities was exhausted in seven years' time and they ultimately, but reluctantly, sanctioned the building plans. The construction of the three buildings, therefore, started under the supervision of the architect in the year 2000 i.e. seven years after the building plans had been submitted, and could be completed by the year 2002.

This has been a long-standing story with many people of Delhi for several decades. They, of course, eventually did pay the necessary bribes and were able to construct their buildings. Some, however, are not willing to pay bribe, and opt for going ahead with the construction of their buildings without complying with the formality of getting the building plans sanctioned before starting the construction. I am given to understand that more than half of the buildings, particularly in the eastern part of Delhi, which have come up in the recent decades are without such sanctions and could, therefore, be regarded as illegal constructions liable to demolition.

In fact, many enterprising colonisers have been purchasing vast agricultural lands from the farmers and getting a layout prepared with proper roads, etc., and selling the plots carved out in the layout to people wanting land to construct houses for themselves. A large part of East Delhi has grown in this manner.

There is a colony in East Delhi, adjacent to Noida, known as New Ashok Nagar. It has a large number of shops and houses with proper roads, and has come up because of the efforts of some such enterprising colonisers. The commercial as well as the residential buildings have been constructed by the people who purchased these plots.

Realizing that such colonies do come up, although in contravention of the law, and are properly designed colonies, the Government of India decided that there should be a scheme for regularization of such colonies. In order to regularize such unauthorized colonies, which could be done without detriment to the public interest, the Parliament enacted the National Capital Territory of Delhi Laws (Special Provisions) Act, 2007. The preamble to the Act states as follows:

WHEREAS there had been phenomenal increase in the population of the National Capital Territory of Delhi owing to migration and other factors resulting in tremendous pressure on land and infrastructure leading to encroachment or unauthorised developments which are not in consonance with the concept of planned development as provided in the Master Plan of Delhi, 2001 and the relevant Acts and building byelaws made thereunder;

AND WHEREAS the Master Plan of Delhi, 2001 has been extensively modified and notified by the Central Government on 7th February, 2007 with the perspective for the year 2021 keeping in view the emerging new dimensions in urban development vis-a-vis the social, financial and other ground realities;

AND WHEREAS the Central Government has considered and finalised a policy regarding regularisation of unauthorised colonies, village abadi area and its extension, as existed on the 31st day of March, 2002 for which the guidelines are being framed;

AND WHEREAS it is expedient to have a law in terms of the Master Plan of Delhi, 2021, in continuation of the said Act for a period up to 31st December, 2008 to provide temporary relief and to minimise avoidable hardships and irreparable loss to the people of the National Capital Territory of Delhi against any action by the concerned agency in respect of persons covered by the policies referred to above which are expected to be finalised within the period so extended.

Delhi Paramedical and Management Institute (DPMI) is a registered Institute and is affiliated to the Punjab Technical University. The Institute was established in the year 1996 with the objective of providing quality Paramedical and Technical Management education to students who had studied either up to Class Ten or Class Twelve.

Most of India lives in villages and practises agriculture. This obviously had limitations as to the number of people who can be employed in the field and, hence, as the family size grew, new members ventured to the cities to find jobs. But these would be menial low-paying jobs. It was thus necessary to impart them relevant skills so that they could find better paying jobs and that was the idea behind DPMI.

The medical education normally provides for producing doctors and requires at least an M.B.B.S. degree. However, each doctor requires a team of trained paramedical staff to provide assistance to him either in hospitals or in private clinics. In order to provide this assistance in a proper manner, they need to be given necessary training for that job and also a proper certificate on completion of their course of training. The DPMI, therefore, in this field, introduced courses at two levels, a diploma course of one-year duration and a degree course of three-year duration. It is pretty similar in other fields like hospitality, where people are required to attend to various jobs in hotels, including the role of chefs, who could cook different international cuisines. In this field too, they have introduced courses at two levels—a diploma and a degree one. The DPMI, therefore, has been doing a great job and every year about a thousand students graduate in different fields from this institute.

The Institute constructed its main building many years back on some plots in New Ashok Nagar. In 2010, in view of the expansion of its activities, the Institute required additional accommodation and, therefore, it purchased a new plot B-28, New Ashok Nagar, measuring 340 square yards which was situated right in front of the Institute's main building. This plot already had a building in which one Jayaprakash Gupta was living who had constructed it in the year 1996. Since his house was a pretty large one, a part of it was let out by Gupta to a tenant from whom he was receiving a comparatively handsome rent. The tenant was in possession of telephone, water, and electricity bills, house tax receipts, etc., which were being paid by him from 1996 to 2010. The DPMI, therefore, purchased this building at a high price and carried out renovation work to make it suitable for its pathological, radiology computer laboratories, and a library of the Institute. This renovated building was situated on the main road which ran in front of the entire colony.

As the renovated building looked new, and the DDA felt that the road in front of the colony, being a Master Plan road, needed to be widened, it was necessary to demolish all the buildings situated on the main road and started doing so selectively. When the officials of the DDA approached the Institute and told its Director that within a few days they were going to demolish their new building, which was on the main road, he approached my office to look into the matter.

On studying the whole case, I not only found that there was clear evidence that a large house was already in existence since 1996, but also that the plea of the DDA that they needed this land to widen the road running in front of the colony, was also bogus because at one part of the road, a metro station had already been constructed which was already in operation and only the existing width of the road had been provided and, therefore, in that portion of the road, where the station has been constructed, the road could not be widened without demolishing the station—which was impossible. I also found that after the existing road, there was a canal and beyond the canal, a wide road had already been constructed in order to cater for the traffic which could have used the road in front of the colony. It was clear, therefore, that after the metro station had been constructed the authorities had altered their original plan of widening this road and had carried out the alternative plan of providing a wide road on the other side of the parallel canal. I, therefore, got a Writ Petition drafted to be filed in the Delhi High Court against the demolition.

It was provided under Section 3 of the Act that notwithstanding anything contained in any relevant law or any rules, regulations or byelaws made thereunder, the Central Government shall before the expiry of the Act take all possible measures to finalize norms, policy guidelines and feasible strategies to deal with the problem of encroachment or unauthorized development. It was also provided in Section 3 that a scheme containing guidelines for regularization of unauthorized colonies as existed on 31 March 2002 and where construction took place even beyond that date and up to 8 February 2007 would be covered by the policy guidelines, and the strategies to be prepared before the expiry of the Act.

Sub-section (2) of Section 3 provided that subject to the provisions contained in sub-section (1) and notwithstanding any judgement, decree or order of any court, status quo as on the 1 January 2006 in respect of encroachment or unauthorized development which existed on the 31 March 2002 and where construction took place even beyond that date and up to 8 February 2007 shall be maintained.

However, there was an exception in Section 4 which provided

that the provisions of the Act would not apply in respect of unauthorized development on public land or removal of unauthorized colonies in accordance with the relevant policies approved by the Central Government for clearance of land required for specific public projects. The Act also provided for framing of regulations and giving of directions by the Central Government.

Although the Act was for a limited period, by successive Acts of 2009 and 2011 onwards, the provisions were re-enacted and the period of maintenance of status quo with the exceptions as already mentioned was further continued for several years.

As the demolition of the DPMI building by the DDA was scheduled to take place on 19 July 2011, the case required urgent orders of the High Court. Therefore, the Writ Petition was prepared and when it was ready to be filed on 18 July 2011, it had to be mentioned before the Chief Justice of the Delhi High Court for urgent hearing on the same date. The Chief Justice was kind enough to accept the request for urgent hearing and directed that Justice Rajiv Sahai Endlaw should hear the matter the same day after the lunch break was over.

The Writ Petition was accordingly heard by Justice Endlaw on the same date, which was 18 July 2011, and a detailed order was issued. The order stated that the petition had been received after lunch on urgent mentioning and it sought to restrain the Respondent DDA from taking action for demolition of property No.B-28 in New Ashok Nagar, Delhi, admittedly an unauthorized colony. It was also noted in the order that the counsel for the Respondent DDA had appeared on advance notice and he stated that demolition action had been scheduled for 19 July 2011 only for construction to be carried out in the property after February 2011. The DDA counsel also stated that the constructions fall in the right-of-way to be covered by a proposed widening of the Master Plan road and, therefore, was also covered by the exceptions provided in the Act itself.

As the contention of the DDA was controverted by the Petitioner on facts, Justice Endlaw appointed a Court Commissioner to visit and inspect the property on the following day in the presence of the Deputy Director of DDA and the Director of the Petitioner Institute. Lawyer Ms Shakun Parashar was appointed as Commissioner for the purpose, and who was also to look at the property photographs being shown to the court. The Writ Petition was directed to be listed on 02 August 2011 and it was directed that till then no action for demolition of the property shall be taken. It was this interim order which saved the Petitioner Institute from the threat of demolition and which was extended from time to time by the court. The Court Commissioner had filed a report in which it was stated that when she inspected the property, no fresh construction was going on. She also stated that it was difficult to make out by inspecting the property whether any new construction has been made post February 2011.

The DDA filed a formal counter affidavit in court, in which they stated that even if the constructions had been made prior to February 2007, which was the cut-off date provided in the Act, the exception under Section 4 also applied as the land on which the building stood was required for widening of a Master Plan road and in that connection, they referred to Clause 3.3 of the regulations of 2008 which provided that unauthorized colonies which fall in the area of a proposed Master Plan road would not be considered for regularization. We thereupon filed our rejoinder affidavit in which we first dealt with the contention of the DDA for relying on some photographs that these were new constructions. In regard to this plea, this is what we stated in the fourth paragraph of our rejoinder affidavit:

First of all, it is submitted that the DDA has taken this Hon'ble Court for a ride by placing photographs which do not relate to the property of the Petitioner Institute. The DDA has annexed the photographs of the plots adjacent to the property in dispute (i.e. Plot Nos.25, 26 & 27 whereas the plot no. over which the Petitioner's building is situated is 28) in order to mislead this Hon'ble Court that there was no such construction as is being claimed by the Petitioner on or before 23.02.2011. The Petitioner is filing photographs of those very plots, taken on 16th August 2011, which on being compared to the photographs of the DDA clearly show that the DDA has placed wrong photographs which have nothing to do with the building in dispute. Copies of the latest photographs of the plots adjacent to the property in dispute are annexed hereto as Annexure A. The Petitioner is also annexing the Map prepared by RWA of New Ashok Nagar as Annexure B.

We also stated in the fifth paragraph of the rejoinder affidavit as below:

It is submitted that there was already existing a house consisting of two big rooms apart from one kitchen and one toilet since 1996. The said house was big enough to accommodate the family of five members of the erstwhile owner as well as four members of the tenant which is apparent from the ration card of the erstwhile owner and voter identity cards of the tenant and his wife. The Petitioner is also filing the income tax return of the erstwhile owner which shows that in 2003–2004, he was getting Rs.2,500 as rent from one room which was rented out by him. Copies of the ration card of the erstwhile owner, voter identity cards of his tenants as well as IT return for one financial year of the erstwhile owner are annexed hereto as Annexure C(Colly).

So far as the DDA's main contention that the land was required for a public project i.e. widening of the existing 13.5-metre road to make it 45-metre wide, we dealt with this plea in the sixth paragraph as below:

> The DDA's main contention is that as the land is required for public project i.e. widening of existing 13.5 meter wide road to make it 45 meter wide road, the Petitioner Institute is not entitled to any kind of protection either under National Capital Territory of Delhi Laws (Special Provisions) Act, 2011 or DDA Regulations 2008 for Regularisation of Unauthorised Colonies. The DDA is relying upon a map of the Zonal Plan which envisages a road of 45 meter wide connecting road leading to Gazipur to the Road going from Mayur Vihar to Noida. However, the facts on the ground show that the latest demolition drive of the DDA for road widening is completely devoid of any rationale or planning. In fact, the ground realities suggest that the plan of the DDA for building 45 meter wide road over the said area, which must have been prepared long back, must be deemed to have been abandoned. Some of the facts suggesting aforementioned conclusion by the Petitioner for consideration of this Hon'ble Court are mentioned below:
>
> In order to implement the plan of making 45 meter wide road under Master Plan (Zonal Plan), the DDA will have to demolish not only large number of private houses, two big temples (one of them being an ancient temple) but also a big government school and the Metro Station of New Ashok Nagar which also fall on the same stretch Zonal Plan that when a 45 meter wide road was envisaged, there was no metro station over there. However, now a big metro station has come up over the said stretch and which makes the implementation of the plan of building a 45 meter wide

road over the said land without demolishing the major part of the Metro Station impossible. The Metro Station, which is operational since 2009, is approx. 300 meters away from the Petitioner Institute. It would be pertinent hereto mention that on one side of the proposed road is New Ashok Nagar and on another side, there is big boundary wall separating a strip of land which was given to the UP Government by the Delhi Government over which now a canal has been built by them.

As mentioned above, the proposed road is supposed to connect a road leading to Gazipur with a road between Mayur Vihar and Noida. The Master Plan or Zonal Plan, which contains the provision for the said road and which is being relied upon by the DDA does not provide for any other road in vicinity of the said road connecting the same two roads. However, as on date, there are already two parallel roads existing, one of them is 30 meter wide with a divider for two way traffic which connects not only same two roads, but it also provides direct connectivity to the DND Toll Bridge which makes it much more convenient for traffic coming from South Delhi or Ring Road. These two parallel roads are hardly few meters away from the proposed road but the Map on which the DDA is relying does not show them at all. Despite the fact there are already two parallel roads which cater to the same traffic for which the DDA is planning to widen third road, the DDA has started demolishing private buildings on the pretext of requirement of the land for the public project knowing fully well that this widening is otherwise also not feasible at all in the wake of construction of the Metro Station. It is really amazing that the DDA has unleashed this demolition drive for the project which is not only now not required but also not feasible which clearly reflects poorly on the planning of the DDA as well as its execution. Copies of the Map as contained in Master Plan/Zonal Plan and a Map of the said area prepared by the Petitioner Institute are annexed hereto as Annexure D (Colly).

In view of these clear facts we had placed before the court, the petition had become unanswerable and on behalf of the DDA, their counsel kept on having the matter adjourned from time to time for several years and finally on 6 June 2012, the DDA issued a gazette notification under Section 57 of the Delhi Development Act, 1957 in which it was said that:

GNCTD will finalise the boundaries of each identified colony having more than 50% built-up area by superimposing the satellite/aerial survey images as obtained in 2007 on the layout plan submitted by the Residents Welfare Society. Clause 5.4 of the notification further provided that after fixing the boundaries on layout plan as in para 5.3, GNCTD will forward the layout plan to Local Body. Simultaneously GNCTD will issue orders regularizing the colony as per the boundaries fixed after recovery of cost of land on behalf of land owning agency in respect of colonies on public land to be credited to the account of land owning agency. Thereafter, DDA will affect change in land use and local body concern shall approve the Layout Plan. Development charges as determined will be collected by Local Body concern from the Residents Societies/ Individual.

Thereafter, on 4 September 2012, an order was made by the GNCTD stating that:

Government had been able to identify 895 unauthorised colonies located without any forest and ridge areas and protected area under the provisions of Ancient Monuments and Archaeological Sites and Remains Act 1958 and also not posing any hindrance to the provisions of infrastructural facilities under the Master Plan 2021 as eligible for regularization under the said Regulations 2008 and the boundaries of each identified colony have been finalized under Clause 5.3 of the Regulations 2008 as amended on 06.06.2012. These identified unauthorized colonies are given in Annexures I and II to this order as follows.

They finally stated:

Now, therefore, in exercise of the powers delegated under Clause 5.4 of the regulations the GNCTD hereby orders that the above named colonies Annexure will stand regularized as per boundaries finalized as follows.

The list of unauthorized colonies so regularized included at item 29 New Ashok Nagar, Chilla Saroda, Bangar, Delhi-96. We also filed a copy of the map fixing the boundaries of the areas regularized which showed that the disputed building of the DPMI fell within the boundaries of the regularized colony, New Ashok Nagar. So, these notifications along with the boundary map were also filed with the court along with an additional affidavit. After the issuance of the order regularizing New Ashok Nagar with the boundaries as specified, the Writ had really become infructuous and it was not necessary to take the Court's time on the same. We, therefore, decided to make a request to withdraw the petition reserving our right to file a fresh petition if the need ever arose and if in spite of the regularization notification, some authorities wanted to demolish the Institute. After the withdrawal of the petition, nothing has happened and the Institute is going from strength to strength.

Now, in retrospect, it appears that many of the buildings had been needlessly demolished by the DDA on that very strip of land. I leave it to the imagination of the readers as to why the authorities selectively started demolishing certain properties whenever they could find some excuse to do so irrespective of whether it was in public interest to do so or not.

This case also illustrates how the constitutional authority of the High Courts under Article 226 of the Constitution, when wisely used, serves a great purpose. It could enhance the faith of the people in these institutions. Whenever a client gets relief against imminent disaster, through a lawyer's help, he gets so obligated to the lawyer that he wants to do anything for him/her. The directors of the DPMI whom I find to be enterprising, honest, hard-working and competent people, and who are rendering a great service to the poor through their Institute, keep meeting me fairly often. Every year on my birthday, they organize blood donation camps on their premises in which a large number of their students and staff donate blood. They are also always willing to offer whatever help is possible for important social causes. One of my Nepali cooks' daughter was admitted into their three-year degree course of hospitality management—from which she graduated with flying colours. When she moved to Australia after marriage, she got a very well-paying job as a junior chef in one of the five star hotels at Adelaide. I regard her career as a testimony of the great work that the DPMI is doing in this field. I have been told by the people at the Institute that the Skill Development Corporation of India, which has been recently established, has also found their work to be of a high order and is assisting them in expanding in many other States in the country. This shows that if an institution is run by people who are honest, devoted, and hard-working, it could go a long way in fulfilling the ambitions of that institution.

17
THE PATENT CASE OF NOVARTIS

This chapter is in respect of the most important patent case that I have argued in my professional career—the case of the patentability of a cancer drug. I appeared on behalf of Novartis, a Swiss Company and one of the largest companies in the field of drug research in the world. I was instructed to represent Novartis in this litigation by the biggest intellectual property firm—Remfry & Sagar, headed by Dr Vidyasagar, a very able and enterprising person. I appeared on his behalf in Madras High Court as well as the Intellectual Property Appellate Board to which the Madras High Court ultimately transferred all the cases. The matter had gone before the Appellate Board continuously for several weeks and finally I was able to secure a judgement in favour of Novartis from the Appellate Board on all the three major points involved in the case. But, on one of the points I was not able to convince them; so on that point, they gave a verdict against Novartis.

Against this verdict of the Appellate Board on the point on which they decided against Novartis, we filed an appeal in the Supreme Court and at the stage of admission, I argued it and got the appeal admitted.

However, before the appeal came up for final hearing, for

some reason, Novartis decided to drop Remfry & Sagar as its briefing attorney and engaged another firm. They, however, were keen that I should continue to represent Novartis in the Supreme Court also and argue their appeal. However, I felt that since I had been briefed by Remfry & Sagar, it would not be ethically right for me to continue to represent Novartis on being briefed by their new briefing attorney firm, particularly as there did not appear to be any good reason for Novartis to abandon Remfry & Sagar. I, therefore, declined to represent Novartis in the appeal in the Supreme Court at the time of the final hearing and their new briefing attorney firm had to engage another senior counsel. Ultimately, the Supreme Court gave a decision not only approving the decision of the Appellate Board on the points on which it had decided against Novartis, but also overruling the three major points on which the Appellate Board had given its decision in favour of Novartis, leading to Novartis losing on all the four points in the case.

Before I started dictating the contents of this chapter, I was wondering whether people, who would read my memoirs, would be interested at all in reading this chapter dealing with a technically difficult legal case. It then occurred to me that every part of a memoir may not be of interest to every section of the reading public and, therefore, they were free to read the chapters of their choice. Also, I felt that many lawyers, particularly the young enterprising ones, were quite likely to feel interested in the intricacies of the patent law. I have, therefore, decided to include this chapter as well.

Many new cancer drugs are extremely expensive, which can only be afforded by the ultra-rich when one does not have any medical insurance. But medical insurance for covering cancer can also be pretty expensive. In the field of patents for drugs, even though the life of a patent is only twenty years, it is possible for new pharmaceutical companies to analyse the drug in regard to its composition by breaking it down and then producing that drug by any other method at a much cheaper price—this is called 'generic drug'. These pharmaceutical companies, if the drug does not enjoy a patent even for twenty years, would be able to secure huge profits by producing and selling it at a fraction of the price at which the inventor of the drug sells them internationally. This is the reason why there is a lot of litigation about the patentability of a new drug in which several senior counsels are asked to appear for long periods.

The justification for patentability of drugs is on account of the fact that even after years of extensive research, which can be extremely painstaking, and a large sum of money invested— before a drug can be finally approved for use, if such a product is not patented, anybody can get it at very little cost and the original inventor of the drug would not be able to recover even the costs of his research and, therefore, no incentive would be left for carrying on with the expensive and painstaking research in the development of new drugs.

This is the reason behind the international treaty known as TRIPS, which is the international agreement on Trade-Related Aspects of Intellectual Property Rights. This is the treaty to which a very large number of countries in the world, including India, are party and are bound by its provisions so entered into in 1965. While TRIPS provides for many kinds of intellectual property rights, like copyright, trademarks, industrial licence, its most important aspect relates to patents and is dealt with in Article 27 of the treaty. This Article deals with patentable subject matter, rights conferred by a patent, conditions on patent application, exceptions to rights conferred, other use without authorization of the right holder, revocation, and forfeiture of a patent and term of protection, which is twenty years.

In the patentable subject matter, it is provided that patents shall be available for any inventions, whether products or processes, in all fields of technology, provided that they are new, involve an inventive step and are capable of industrial application.

Normally, when a nation enters into an international treaty and is bound by its provisions, it has to take action which is in conformity with the treaty. However, if its actions, legislative or executive, do not conform to the treaty, action can be taken by it only in a world forum at the United Nations-level. This is the reason that when the Indian Parliament enacts a law, which is not in conformity to an international treaty, it cannot be struck down on the ground that it is violating a treaty to which India is a party. The legislation enacted by the Parliament, notwithstanding its being in conflict with the international treaty, will prevail so far as any Indian institutions, including the courts are concerned. The Patent Act of 1970 was enacted by the Parliament long before the TRIPS treaty.

After the TRIPS treaty was entered into, since it was not possible for member countries to take action immediately in respect of provisions contained in the TRIPS treaty, Part 6 of TRIPS provided for transitional arrangement in which it was provided that no member shall be obliged to apply the provisions of the treaty before the expiry of a general period of one year following the date of the WTO agreement came into force.

In respect of the developing countries, which included India, it was provided that a member is entitled to delay for a further period of four years after the date of application as defined in Part 1 of the provisions of this treaty other than Articles 3, 4, and 5. It was further provided in Clause 4 of Article 65 relating to transitional arrangement that 'to the extent that a developing country member is obliged by this agreement to extend product patent protection to areas of technology not so protectable in its territory on the general date of application of this agreement for that member, as defined in Part 2, it may delay the application of the provisions of product patent of Section 5 of Part 2 to such areas of technology for an additional period of 5 years.' As at the time when the TRIPS agreement came into effect, the Indian Patents Act by Section 5 had excluded product patentability for medicines and confined patentability of medicines only in regard to processes, the Indian Parliament had, ten years from 1995, to introduce patentability of the drugs per se irrespective of the processes by which they were produced. Therefore, the Parliament had to amend the Patents Act in 2005, which it did by the Patents (Amendment) Act, 2005 with effect from 1 January 2005 to bring it in line with the TRIPS agreement and since that time, any product became patentable and, therefore, once a new drug was rightly patented for twenty years, no other pharmaceutical company could produce that drug even by employing a different process as the product itself enjoyed a patent.

This was the reason why when Novartis applied for a patent in respect to its new drug, 'beta Crystalline Form of Imatinib Mesylate', its application, when advertised, was opposed by five pharmaceutical companies. The Controller of Patents, by its order dated 25 January 2006, allowed the opposition to the patent application of Novartis by all the five pharmaceutical companies and this order of the Controller was challenged by Novartis first in the Madras High Court from where ultimately, the case was transferred to the Intellectual Property Appellate Board at Chennai for being disposed of on merits as the dispute fell within the jurisdiction of the Appellate Board. The three-member Appellate Board heard extensive arguments at great length, not only on behalf of Novartis, but also on behalf of the opposing pharmaceutical companies, who were interested in manufacturing the equivalent of that drug by a different process which they could do very cheaply and not only sell their products in India, but also export them to many other countries. Let me mention here that even the generic drugs which were to be produced by these companies were going to be comparatively cheaper, but in absolute terms they were also going to be very expensive and beyond the reach of even the lower middle classes, not to say of the poor people of the country.

Under the Patents Act, as amended in 2005, a patent could only be granted for an invention. An invention was defined under Section 2(1) (j) in the following terms:

> 'Invention' means a new product or process involving an inventive step and capable of industrial application.

The expression 'inventive step' has been defined under Section 2(1) (ja) in the following terms:

> 'Inventive step' means a feature of an invention that involves technical advance as compared to the existing knowledge or having economic significance or both and that makes the invention not obvious to a person skilled in the art.

Under Section 2(1) (l), an invention can be regarded as new if it has not been anticipated by publication in any document or used in the country or elsewhere in the world before the date of filing of patent application. Clause (l) reads as under:

> 'New invention' means any invention or technology which has not been anticipated by publication in any document or used in the country or elsewhere in the world before the date of filing of patent application with complete specification, i.e. the subject matter has not fallen in public domain or that it does not form part of the state of the art.

One of the objections to the grant of patent for the new drug beta Crystalline Form of Imatinib Mesylate was that in 1993 patent of an invention relating to 'Pyrimidine Derivatives' and process for the preparation thereof was granted for the product. The abstract stated that these compounds can be used in the therapy of tumour diseases. The 1993 patent was in respect of a large number of compounds and pharmaceutically acceptable salt thereof which had anti-cancer properties.

However, in order to produce drugs which could be beneficially used for cancer treatment, it required another long period of painstaking research that a particular salt of that group in a particular form would have advantageous properties and could be selected as drug. The principle involved has been called the 'principle of selection patent' which has been adopted by the courts and also finds mention under Section 3(d) of the Indian Patents Act of 1970.

Section 3(d) provides as follows:

The mere discovery of a new form of a known substance which does not result in the enhancement of the known efficacy of that substance or the mere discovery of any new property or new use for a known substance or of the mere use of a known process, machine or apparatus unless such known process results in a new product or employs at least one new reactant.

Explanation: For the purposes of this clause, salts, esters, ethers, polymorphs, metabolites, pure form, particle size, isomers, mixtures of isomers, complexes, combinations and other derivatives of known substance shall be considered to be the same substance, unless they differ significantly in properties with regard to efficacy.

It was contented by us on behalf of Novartis that for the purposes of Section 3(d), imatinib-free base had in fact been prepared and tested in preclinical studies, including tests demonstrating the inhibition of the growth of human bladder carcinoma cells in isolation and in mice as described in the 1993 patent. The patent merely suggested the possibility of its being converted into various kinds of salts, which had neither been prepared nor tested for their qualities. If imatinib must be considered to be the known substance for the purpose of section 3(d), then the beta crystalline form of a salt namely imatinib mesylate cannot at all be treated as mere discovery of a new form of a known substance. Beta crystalline form of imatinib mesylate cannot possibly be described as a new form of imatinib-free base.

It was shown that beta crystalline form of imatinib mesylate had the advantage that its flow properties were substantially more favourable than those of the a-crystal form. This crystal form has the further advantage of being thermodynamically more stable at temperatures below 140°C although the beta crystal form was less hygroscopic than the a-crystal form and thus stored better and was easier to process.

In an affidavit filed before the Controller, one Dr Manley had stated that the physical properties of imatinib-free base and imatinib mesylate differed in that the free base was only very slowly soluble while imatinib mesylate in its beta crystal form was very soluble in water. The attendant advantages were also simultaneously described in the affidavit. It was, therefore, claimed that if a drug in a particular form is very effective over the other known forms, each of the forms can be claimed by way of patent rights. It was pointed out by us that in a cancer drug, bio-availability was a very important feature of the drug because if in a particular form the bio-availability can be enhanced, it was possible to give lower doses of the drug which could be equally effective so far as the disease was concerned and yet the lower doses would reduce the adverse effects of that drug to a very significant extent. This, therefore, enhances the efficacy of the drug in its present beta crystalline form and meets the requirements of Section 3(d) fully.

The Appellate Board gave a very long judgement on the issue of 1993 patent covering Gleevec. Beta form of imatinib mesylate thus stood anticipated. The Board held that it could not be said that the crystal form was known or anticipated before the priority date of the impugned application for a patent and, therefore, was decided in favour of Novartis.

In this judgement, the Appellate Board stated:

The main issues raised in the appeals are:

1. Priority date
2. Novelty/Anticipation
3. Inventive step/non-obviousness
4. Selection Patent
5. Section 3(d) of the Act

On priority date, the Appellate Board decision was expected and it was held that Novartis was fully justified and entitled to get the convention priority date 18.07.1997 under the amended section 133 of the Act. On the question of Novelty/Anticipation, the Appellate Board held:

> We thus, observe that none of the Respondents could establish 'anticipation' of the instant impugned invention as a product the beta form of imatinib mesylate, a pharmaceutical composition comprising the same and a claim for the process for preparing the said beta form of imatinib mesylate as given in the statement of claims. Use claims being not patentable are excluded for consideration. We thus reverse the impugned orders of R8 on the ground of 'anticipation'.

On the question of inventive step/non-obviousness, the Appellate Board held:

> Thus, we cannot agree with any of the Respondents that the Appellant's alleged invention lacks inventive step. IPER and the decision of the Board of Appeals and Interferences of USPTO also upheld existence of inventive step. We, thus reverse the R8's decision on inventive step in his impugned orders.

On Selection Patent also, the Appellate Board decided in favour of Novartis by holding that:

> Thus, here, the Appellant has demonstrated the inventive step not only by the classical way but also by way of 'selection'.

On the last question, namely relating to Section 3(d) of the Act, however, the Appellate Board ruled against Novartis by holding that 'bio-availability is not the same as therapeutic efficacy.' It held that:

> By demonstrating enhanced bio-availability of 30% which also is obvious, because of increased solubility of the salt in water the Appellant could not show any actual enhancement of known efficacy for its subject compound with respect to either imatinib or imatinib mesylate as the known substance.

Thus, it finally held that 'By not satisfying section 3(d) of the Act would mean that acclaim for beta crystalline form of imatinib mesylate and a pharmaceutical composition containing the same as products are not patentable under [Section 3(e)] of the Act.' But a patent on the said process described in the application could not be denied to Novartis. Finally, the operative part of the order was:

We, therefore, dispose of the present appeals and remand back the impugned application to the Patent Office (Chennai) with the direction to the Controller to grant a patent expeditiously to the Appellant with the Swiss Convention priority on record subject to the impugned specification being amended by the Appellant restricting the statement of claims to process claims only subject to the office objections raised in the first examination report dated 17th March 2005 being complied with as per the requirements of the law.

It was our submission that on the question of Section 3(d), the Appellate Board's conclusion was incorrect because if a particular cancer drug enhances bio-availability by 30 per cent, it means that a smaller dose can be effectively used for treating cancer and thus immensely reducing the adverse side effects which are so common in chemotherapy by cancer drug. This could not but be regarded as an enhanced therapeutic efficacy. If, on account of 30 per cent higher bio-availability, you can reduce the dose of a drug, which has very strong adverse side effects, this, in my opinion, is nothing but an enhancement of therapeutic efficacy.

However, as I have said above, the Supreme Court decided it against Novartis. The Supreme Court does not appear to have appreciated that the Patents Act has a provision for a compulsory licence being granted by the Controller to any person who desires to manufacture a drug, which is covered by a patent. The Controller has the power under Section 84 of the Patents Act to grant a compulsory licence to any person interested at any time after the expiration of three years from the date of the grant of a patent, if the patent invention is not available to the public at a reasonably affordable price.

Under Section 90, the terms and conditions of a compulsory licence have to be determined by the Controller who is required to endeavour to secure that the royalty and other remuneration, if any, reserved to the patentee is reasonable, having regard to the nature of invention, expenditure incurred by the patentee in making the invention or in developing it and obtaining a patent and keeping it in force and other relevant factors.

In my view this is a very useful provision, which if used properly will balance the interest of extensive research in discovering and preparing new effective drugs after costly research and needs of the humanity for that drug which could be made available to it at comparatively reasonable prices.

18
MY TWILIGHT YEARS

My father detested being called old. And so do I, which is why the title of this chapter is not 'Getting Old'. I am now in my 93rd year. As you advance in years, your mental and physical faculties get weaker. Fortunately, my mental faculties are fresh as ever, but my physical ones are undoubtedly getting affected. I almost constantly suffer from shoulder pain due to a frozen shoulder in spite of regular yoga sessions with my teacher, Akhilesh Pandey, and regular physiotherapy treatment. My hearing has been impaired and even with the sophisticated hearing aids, many times I am not able to comprehend what the judges are saying to me in a court and my junior has to keep on communicating to me what is being said. I also have to use a walking stick for my short morning walks.

However, I still argue some important cases in the Supreme Court or the Delhi High Court and, rarely though, even outside of Delhi, like Mumbai or Bengaluru. But I go to court only on the days that I have a case. Otherwise I stay at home. No human being can sit idle, otherwise he will sink into depression. Almost every morning during my morning walk, I meet my friend and editor, P.C. Verma, former principal of Delhi University's Hindu College at his residence as he does not move out of his house due to his weak knees. He is very fond of buying and reading books and shares them with his friends. He keeps suggesting interesting books to me to read and I have thus also become a voracious reader over the years. I have the habit of reading books word by word, omitting nothing. In the last couple of years, I have read the almost 1,500 pages long *War and Peace* by Leo Tolstoy, the great American novel, *Gone with the Wind* by Margaret Mitchell, Feroze Gandhi's biography, *The Forgotten Gandhi*, and many other good books, the last of them being *Mr and Mrs Jinnah: The Marriage that Shook India*. It was the tragic story of the life of Ruttee Petit—an extremely pretty and vivacious daughter of the richest Parsi Baron in Bombay, Sir Dinshaw Petit. She fell in love at the young age of sixteen with Muhammad Ali Jinnah, twenty-four years senior to her, but a great lawyer and politician, higher in stature than even Mahatma Gandhi at that time. The pretty Ruttee fled home without the knowledge of her parents, converted to Islam in a mosque and had a nikah with Jinnah the following day. Later in life she became so miserable in life that on her 29th birthday, she committed suicide. It is a story so well told by its author that it leaves a deep impression on you.

Being surrounded by a loving family, particularly my grandchildren, I continue to pass my days happily. One of these days, an incident which happened as long back as 1947 came to my mind. My father Vishwamitra had gone to see Sir Tej Bahadur Sapru—the doyen of the Indian Bar. After finishing the matter for which my father had gone to him, Sir Tej said to my father:

> *Vishwamitter, maine apni zindagi me bahut kamaya lekin bahut kharch bhi kiya, kuchh bachaya nahin. Ab main jab maroonga to mere pote kahenge ki sale ne itna kamaya par sab khud hi kha gaya, hamare liye kuchh nahin chorha. Mujhe sirf isi bat ka dukh hai. Jawaharlal do din me mere pass aane wale hain. Meri nani ne bahut pahale do bagh dilli*

*me kharide the, kuchh roz hue ek coloniser aya tha aur kah
raha tha ki agar aap sarkar se colonisation ke permission
dilwa den to hum apko tees lakh dekar wo zamin kharid
sakte haim. Main Jawaharlal se kahoonga. Agar wo maan
gaye to main do do lakh ke cheques har pote our poti ko
dekqar chain se mar sakoonga.*

Essentially, Sir Tej told my father said that the former had earned
a lot in his life but spent most of it and now if he were to die then
he won't be able to leave anything for his grandsons and they will
curse him for that. He also told my father that Jawaharlal would
be visiting him in a few days and that Sir Tej would request him
for a permission to colonize a piece of land that he owned, so
that he could sell that land off to a colonizer and then gift the
proceeds to his grandson and then die in peace. The permission
did come from the government and Sir Tej got ₹30 lakh. He gave
cheques of ₹2 lakh each to his grandchildren and died in peace
soon thereafter. When I remembered this, I thought to myself
that I had also earned well in my life and I also must emulate Sir
Tej and protect myself from being abused by my grandsons. So, I
made handsome donations to each of my grandchildren so that I
can also die in peace.

When a person crosses the age of three scores and ten, that
is seventy, he begins to feel that he is getting old and does not
know when his end may come. He starts thinking that it is time
to start sharing the joys of his life with his friends and family
by celebrating his birthdays.

I, therefore, publicly celebrated my seventy-fifth birthday in
India Habitat Centre on 11 November 2000. The entire extended
family from my side as well as my late wife's side gathered along
with many from the legal fraternity and other close friends. In
today's busy lives, one meets close relatives and friends only
on occasions like these. Thus birthday celebrations do serve an

important social purpose.

Having migrated to Delhi from Allahabad in 1977, I felt the need to renew my ties with my hometown in the twilight of my life. I, therefore, decided to celebrate my eightieth birthday at Allahabad in our family house—19, Elgin Road. My sister Madhu chalked out a beautiful three-day programme so that family members from far may also have a strong incentive to descend on Allahabad for a few days. There was a big cruise organized on the River Yamuna with dinner being served on the boat, which had come from Kolkata and could seat almost 100 people. Our extended family, including almost all my cousins, had enjoyed three days in Allahabad after many decades. The dinner on the boat was the highlight of the celebrations. The concluding function was a dinner party in which many old friends from Allahabad participated and regaled everybody present with interesting old stories of their interaction with our extended family.

We celebrated my eighty-fifth birthday in Delhi in the enchanting gardens of my niece Seema's beautiful farmhouse in Chhattarpur, where liquor and a winter lunch was enjoyed by a large gathering. The prominent guests included Fali Nariman, Soli Sorabji, Attorney General Vahnavati, Justice J.S. Verma, and Justice Katju. Katju, in fact, rang me up to tell me that he enjoyed a good cigar immensely after a good meal. So, on my way to the farmhouse, I went to a mall to buy the most expensive cigars to ensure that he really enjoyed himself.

Although I had thought that my eight-fifth would be my last birthday to be celebrated as I used to celebrate them only on a five-yearly basis, God willed otherwise and kept me alive for my ninetieth birthday in 2015 as well—which I celebrated in the fountain lawns of the India International Centre. It was a memorable celebration with speeches by Fali Nariman and Ram Jethmalani.

Ram revealed that I had in fact changed the entire course of his life, but at first I could not comprehend what he was saying. He, however, explained that he was only a criminal lawyer from Mumbai and would have remained so but for my defeating Indira Gandhi in the election case in 1975. Her losing that case and the consequent declaration of the Emergency changed the entire course of his life. He became a politician overnight, contested an election, and moved to Delhi. On reflection, I felt it was indeed so. A single event can have such profound effect on a person's life.

Fali Nariman referred to Abou Ben Adhem while referring to Bhushan lawyers. I membered Abou Ben Adhem, may his tribe increase, from my schooldays. He wished that just like Abou Ben Adhem, Bhushan tribe may also increase. In his speech, Fali paid a huge compliment to one of my grandsons, Pawan, who had worked with him as an intern to assist him in demolishing the National Judicial Commission Act in the Supreme Court. He said that Pawan Bhushan in due course was not only going to surpass his father Prashant, but also his grandfather. It was on Fali's recommendation that Pawan got admission to study L.L.M. in the prestigious Georgetown University in Washington DC.

Dr N.P. Asthana, the Advocate General of UP, who lived well into his nineties, once said that longevity has a very sad aspect also. A person has to endure seeing so many close family members and friends die before him and grieve their loss. This is indeed very true.

My wife died almost twenty years ago. One of my younger brothers, who was very close to me, also died thirty years ago. Many of my juniors who became chief Justices have died. Most of my university friends have also passed away. The last of them was Chief Justice H.N. Seth, who was just about three weeks older than me, he too died in October 2017 after having reached the age of ninety-two years. He had been my classmate from childhood in Annie Besant School and we had not only studied law together but had also enrolled for it almost at the same time. I was only one day senior to him as an advocate. On learning of his death, I immediately wrote an article which was published in *The Tribune* with the title: '*Bicharhe Sabhi Bari Bari*' (one by one, everyone got separated). On my last visit to Allahabad in March 2018 for my wife's memorial function in the Allahabad Ladies Club, I met Mrs H.N. Seth who is eighty-eight years old now. She had a married life with Chief Justice Seth for close to seventy years and I can well appreciate her sense of loss in the demise of her beloved husband.

My fellow classmate in intermediate, BSc, and law, R.S. Pathak, who became the Chief Justice of India later, died in 2007. His son Anand Pathak, a distinguished lawyer, forwarded to me a photograph of my friend's wedding in 1955 in which he is sitting in his bridegroom's attire and his six close friends are standing with him. They are Satish Chandra, Amitava Banerji, Teju Sapru, Satyendra Verma, myself, and H.N. Seth. Three of them later became Chief Justices of High Courts—Satish Chandra, Amitava Banerji, and H.N. Seth. Out of the seven of us in the photograph, all have died and only I am alive now. This photograph is appended to this book.

Another important event that took place in December 2017 was the wedding of my youngest daughter Shefali, who as I have already said is a film-maker in Mumbai. At the age of forty-six, she decided to get married to a charming man from Maharashtra by the name of Jayant Somalkar. Coincidentally, Jayant also has a brother named Prashant. So, while Shefali's two brothers are Prashant and Jayant, her husband and brother in-law are also Jayant and Prashant respectively. The wedding celebrations were very festive with two whole eventful days. When some people received the wedding invitations, they were surprised that at this age I was marrying away my daughter. But I told them what I had said to her that she should write on the invitation card: 'Better late than never!'; so as to inspire others who had not yet married but had advanced in years.

When people close to you die it's then that the futility of life dawns on you. But, when I see my grandchildren with happy faces, all the sad thoughts recede into the background and I again feel happy, contented, and blessed.

ACKNOWLEDGEMENTS

I am deeply indebted to several people for *My Second Innings* to have taken shape. Firstly those who had enjoyed my first memoirs, *Courting Destiny*, and some of the reviewers who wrote glowing reviews for it such as former Lok Sabha Speaker Somnath Chatterji, Shri Arun Jaitley, Shri Rajeev Dhawan, Shri Harsh Mander, and all the others. Their reviews in no small measure encouraged me to write again.

I am also indebted to Dr P.C. Verma (former Principal, Hindu College, University of Delhi) to have painstakingly edited what I had written and also to my son Prashant's hardworking and gritty colleague Advocate Siddhartha K. Garg for also editing and giving the book its final shape. I also want to thank the upcoming legal start-up ASAP Law for the beautiful cover photo of the book. ASAP Law is doing an excellent job in providing free videos and coaching for competitive exams like the Judicial Services Exam and UPSC (IAS exam) and also spreading legal awareness among the general public about their legal rights and how to secure them.

I would also like to thank Rupa publications and the team comprising Rudra Sharma and Tanima Saha for publishing the book.

Without the contribution of all these friends this book could not have seen the light of day. I hope my readers will enjoy reading this book as much as they had enjoyed reading *Courting Destiny*.

INDEX